DATE DUE			

THREE MODES OF CRITICISM

Three Modes of Criticism

THE LITERARY THEORIES OF
SCHERER, WALZEL, AND STAIGER

PETER SALM

THE PRESS OF CASE WESTERN RESERVE UNIVERSITY
CLEVELAND
1968

To my wife, June

PREFACE

As a graduate student I had occasionally wondered whether literary theory, by becoming more and more self-conscious, might not tend to remove itself from literature. My first contact with works which might properly be called "criticism of criticism" led to an uncomfortable feeling that a third and yet another level of criticism might develop, so that an infinite series—like the multiple image produced by two opposing mirrors—might be the final result. Related to this discomfort is the widespread notion, usually voiced somewhat plaintively, that criticism is, and ought to be, an art rather than a science. Abstractions, it is pointed out, never quite apply to particular works of literature.

Pedantry and pretentiousness exist in literary scholarship at least as much as in other disciplines; they should be exposed for what they are. But the view that criticism should be "artistic" or "poetic" seems to arise from a confusion of theory and practice. While the two depend on each other for their existence, they remain distinct and distinguishable. Both the art of the literary critic and the thought behind a theory of criticism must have their due, though it is a matter of emphasis rather than of exclusion. I am committed to the idea that literary theory as a philosophic discipline deserves continuing revaluation and that practical criticism cannot but gain from a probing of its theoretical premises.

This study had its start as a doctoral dissertation in 1959 under the tutelage of Professor René Wellek. The second chapter appeared in abbreviated form under the title "Oskar Walzel and the Notion of Reciprocal Illumination in the Arts" in *The Germanic Review* (May, 1961). The revisions since undertaken include the translation

vii

of quoted passages in the text—mostly in German—into English. With few exceptions, I have used my own versions, even when other translations were available, as for example in the case of Heidegger's *Being and Time,* because I found that the point to be demonstrated would emerge more clearly if the passages in the transposed form reflected my own interpretation of them, and I consoled myself with the knowledge that translation necessarily entails interpretation. However, several words and poems quoted in the chapter on Emil Staiger, as well as one passage from Heidegger, were left untranslated because the comments concerning them deal with certain phonemic and structural characteristics of German which, to the best of my knowledge, could not be rendered in translation.

I hope that other substantial revisions have brought this study into line with the present state of criticism and indeed with the state of its author's own development.

PETER SALM

ACKNOWLEDGMENTS

The author is indebted to the following publishers:

Columbia University, for permission to draw upon the author's article "Oskar Walzel and the Notion of Reciprocal Illumination in the Arts," which was published in the May, 1961, issue of *The Germanic Review* and which appears in expanded form in the section on Oskar Walzel in this book.

Akademische Verlagsgesellschaft, for permission to cite from *Gehalt und Gestalt im Kunstwerk des Dichters*, by Oskar Walzel (Berlin-Neubabelsberg, 1923).

Erich Schmidt Verlag, for permission to cite short passages from *Wachstum und Wandel, Lebenserinnerungen von Oskar Walzel*, edited by Carl Enders (Berlin, 1956).

TABLE OF CONTENTS

THREE MODES OF
CRITICISM

INTRODUCTION

Studies dealing with literary theory call for a more international point of view than those dealing directly with literature. A common language and a roughly identical social and political background provide considerable justification for relating literary works to a national or regional context. Yet there is increasing awareness of the limitations of a rigidly national orientation in any critical endeavor, whether applied or explicitly theoretical. While literary movements do have distinctly national colorations, they are penetrated by ideas which have currency in many countries. Poetic and aesthetic theories are justly expected to transcend the special problems of nationality and language.

Works of literature have a way of appearing in their brightest illumination when viewed in their national context. What is peculiarly German in, say, Novalis' *Heinrich von Ofterdinger*, or English in T. S. Eliot's *The Cocktail Party* is of course a legitimate concern. The relevance of national climate and tradition need not be denied. But no matter how pervasively the spirit of a nation may be implicated, there is yet a matrix of poetic principles embedded in literary works which is common to European literature as a whole.

Literary theory which deals with particular works only as illustrations of such basic notions as the relationship of mundane reality to poetry, or with poetic genres, immediately becomes part of a body of aesthetic principles which are general and international by nature. In an analysis of Novalis' scattered critical statements, or of Eliot's essays, national and regional considerations must play a secondary role. Numerous examples could be chosen. It matters little

1

whether the author's theories were conceived as an apologia for his own imaginative writings, or whether he is exclusively a theorist. The literary principles involved must be evaluated on the basis of their own merits. Whether or not Novalis and Eliot actually conformed to their own theories in their poetic works is a question of considerable interest, though not of direct concern to literary theory. While the program outlined by Zola in his "Roman Expérimental" is reflected in his novels in a general way, his theory of scientific naturalism did not account for symbolic, melodramatic, or ironic elements which are also present. Yet naturalism as a program became part of the body of European criticism and had to be dealt with as one of many poetic possibilities.

The fact that the three literary scholars with whom we are primarily concerned form part of the German critical tradition is of relevance to German intellectual history and should not be ignored by proponents of even the most rigidly philosophic poetics. Biographical data may be of similar importance. It must be understood, however, that the inclusion of such background materials cannot be a substitute for an appraisal of the theories themselves.

An understanding of Wilhelm Scherer is undoubtedly enhanced if one realizes that he was an Austrian who was stirred to enthusiasm by the Prussian strides in the direction of German unification under the leadership of Bismarck. Scherer became a Prussian by conviction, which entailed moreover an opposition to Catholicism and religious dogma in general. It is therefore proper to see his bias against Austrian literature in the light of this background. Yet in order to achieve his goal of establishing a new basis for German literary scholarship, he did not hesitate to adopt the ideas of French scientific determinism and of English positivism. His unbounded faith in the methods of natural science was shared by most of his contemporaries.

By the same token, an appraisal of Walzel will be enriched by the information that he was also an Austrian. Quite unlike Scherer, however, Walzel never rejected Catholicism. Religious dogma became an increasingly important and central factor in his life. And accordingly, Walzel's rejection of determinism and the notion of scientific causation in the realm of literature can be seen in a fuller sociological and spiritual context than would be possible without the knowledge of such biographical facts. Walzel's formalistic approach may be regarded as a reaction to the faith of his teachers—most of them prominent members of the Scherer school—in ubiquitous mechanistic causation. He was among the first to see literature as a complex and fairly autonomous system of forms requiring no analysis beyond itself. Catholic dogma was least likely to be endangered by even the fullest implementation of formalism. It was to be preferred even to Dilthey's emphasis on psychology. It should be noted, however, that attempts to elucidate literature by means of concepts originally developed for painting and architecture are neither new nor peculiarly German. They are closely connected with an aesthetic concern which has been important throughout Europe ever since Horace's admonition that a poem should be like a painting.

Emil Staiger is a Swiss whose chief field of interest is German literature, as it had been for Scherer and Walzel. We may point to his deep interest in music and to the fact that he is an accomplished pianist. His special affinity for lyrical poetry, his conception of style as "rhythm," can then be seen as arising naturally from the bent of his personality and the direction of his talent. His predominantly "musical" approach to poetry may be traced to German romanticism and to the principle which M.H. Abrams in *The Mirror and the Lamp* (1953) aptly calls *"ut musica poesis."* Even taking into account the great difficulty of analyzing one's own period, one can claim with confidence that existentialism in its various forms is an important ingredient of the modern intellectual climate. It is a revolt against traditional systems, and within the scope of Staiger's application of Heideggerean principles to literature, an attempt to isolate the categories of existence and temporal modes in creative literature. It is a radical departure from representational thinking and the representational use of language. Words and roots of words become guides to philosophic insights.

Clearly the three scholars represent three succeeding generations: Scherer's important theoretical pronouncements date from the early 1870's and continued to appear until 1886 when he died at the age of forty-five. For Walzel the years between 1910 and 1930 were most productive; Professor Staiger, born in 1908 and now lecturing at the University of Zürich, published his first book in 1939.

No attempt is made in this study, however, to explore the extent to which each of their theories is typical of the generation during which it arose, or, on the other hand, to what degree each was a substantial contribution to the thought and sensibility of a generation. At the same time, the very fact that the three figures were

3

chosen for this investigation is the result of a conviction that they eminently represent major shifts in critical writing between the 1870's and our day.

Historical and biographical facts will be considered whenever they provide us with perspective and focus. This means that critical theories are not evaluated with respect to their historical implications, but rather that I have attempted to examine their premises and methods from a consistently modern point of view. Instead of merely stating that a certain theory was typical of a particular era, we will study the validity of such a theory, in part or *in toto*, for our day. We should be encouraged in our endeavor by the fact that all three of the methods discussed, or at least variations of them, are being practiced today, though the more extreme forms of biographical criticism, such as had been embraced by Scherer's students, appear to have lost most of their authority. Walzel's persistent attempts to develop a vocabulary descriptive of structural elements in literature may be compared to closely related recent trends in American criticism, and Staiger's search for modes of existence, as reflected in literary style, provides strong evidence for the recurring need of ontological revaluation in the field of literary theory.

In our investigations, we will try to keep clearly in mind the distinction between theory and its object, literature. Sidney's famous statement that the poet "nothing affirms and therefore never lieth" is still true. Literary theory, however, is not an art. It deals with aesthetic postulates which may be affirmed or denied. One may properly question the validity of points of theory, and the critic's recourse is not, as in the case of the poet, to the poetic integrity of the written word, but rather to the norms of aesthetic philosophy.

℣ Wilhelm Scherer ℣

Aｌｔｈｏｕｇｈ Sｃｈｅｒｅｒ'ｓ ｒｅｐｕｔａｔｉｏｎ was great among his colleagues and students, it had hardly extended beyond the confines of his profession until the completed *Geschichte der deutschen Litteratur* appeared in the book stores in 1883. The phenomenal success of this book is well known—Scherer himself lived to see three printings of it during the last three years of his life—and its influence on literary historiography and, by extension, on criticism, has been considerable. When thirty years after its first appearance the book had legally entered the public domain, a new publisher promptly availed himself of the opportunity and asked Oskar Walzel to bring Scherer's *History* up to date. The "Scherer-Walzel" which appeared toward the end of 1917 was thus the most comprehensive and popular literary history in Germany; by 1928 the work was in its fourth printing and 29,000 copies had been sold.[1]

Scherer's style is essayistic and uncomplicated. His scholarship was widely acknowledged, and his literary theory, implicit in his history, mirrored the immense confidence of his generation in the efficacy of the methods of natural science. Not since Georg Gottfried Gervinus' *Geschichte der poetischen Nationallitteratur der Deutschen* (Leipzig, 1835) and Julian Schmidt's *Geschichte der deutschen Litteratur seit Lessings Tod* (Leipzig, 1866–67) had there been a literary history which enjoyed popular acceptance comparable to Scherer's work. When he died, at the height of his powers and influence, Scherer left behind a number of disciples, such as Erich Schmidt and August Sauer, who became leaders of the *Scherer-*

---

[1] For a more detailed account, see Oskar Walzel, *Wachstum und Wandel* (Berlin, 1956), p. 183—hereafter cited as *Wachstum und Wandel*.

schule, a most influential group of scholars whose contributions, principally in the field of biography and in the preparation of critical editions, have been invaluable.

Wilhelm Scherer was born in 1841 in the Austrian town of Schönborn. In 1854 he was accepted in the *Akademische Gymnasium* of Vienna, where he soon impressed his teacher Karl Reichel with his capacity to read and absorb such books as Herder's *Ideen*, works by Jacob Grimm, and the literary history of Gervinus. He was imbued with the liberal pan-Germanic principles propounded in the periodical *Grenzbote* by Julian Schmidt. Throughout his life Scherer never ceased to give his fervent political and spiritual support to the idea of a united Germany under the leadership of Prussia.

In 1858 he enrolled in the University of Vienna and attended lectures in German philology given by Bonitz, Vahlen, and Pfeiffer. Dissatisfaction and impatience appear to have set in early, for after the first four semesters he presented himself to the *Germanist* Karl Müllenhoff at the Berlin Academy in order "to learn method" from him. Whether it was primarily Pfeiffer's supposed lack of methodology or that scholar's antipathy to everything emanating from Prussia that irked the young student, is difficult to determine. It is clear, however, that Scherer found a more congenial atmosphere in Berlin and that there he advanced in the direction he desired. In a speech before the Berlin Academy in 1878, he told of how he felt as a student in Berlin and of the exhilaration which he experienced in the presence of admired scholars like the German historian Ranke and the aged philologian Jacob Grimm, revered as a scholar and living link to German romanticism.[2]

During his years of study in Berlin, Scherer joined the table of a group of young scholars who met regularly in a coffee house. Thus he became acquainted with Hermann Grimm, Wilhelm Dilthey, and the jurist A. Boretius. An older person, the literary historian Julian Schmidt whom Scherer had admired in Vienna as one of the contributors to the liberal journal *Grenzbote*, was frequently present, and the historian Theodor Mommsen put in an occasional appearance.[3] It was a group which Julian Schmidt dubbed the "suicide

---

[2] Wilhelm Scherer, *Kleine Schriften*, ed. Konrad Burdach, 2 vols. (Berlin, 1893), I, 212—hereafter cited as *Kleine Schriften*.

[3] For a fuller account, see Erich Rothacker, *Einleitung in die Geisteswissenschaften* (Tübingen, 1920), pp. 137-39.

club," because of the dim view which the young scholars took of their professional and financial future.[4]

In his teacher Müllenhoff, Scherer found a fatherly friend and a stern mentor in rigorous philological method. He became his collaborator in a work called *Denkmäler deutscher Prosa und Poesie vom VII–XII Jahrhundert* (Berlin, 1862), a critical edition and linguistic elucidation of early German poems and small bits of prose. The preparation for this work served Scherer as a basis for his doctoral examination (1862) in Vienna and for his *Habilitation*, which he received two years later.

The first years of Scherer's professional career in Vienna were inauspicious because of the hostility of his former teacher, Franz Pfeiffer, who regarded his pupil's close association with Müllenhoff as a personal affront. Upon receiving the *Denkmäler*, Pfeiffer reportedly exclaimed: "That's the way of the Prussian! Ruthlessly grasping everything, in politics as much as in scholarship." [5] In the quarterly *Germania* founded by Pfeiffer in 1856, considerable space had been devoted to polemics against Lachmann and Müllenhoff, with whose methods Scherer was now closely identified. The *Denkmäler deutscher Prosa* was given a particularly acrimonious review, and a lengthy footnote, signed by Pfeiffer, shows a good deal of personal rancor.[6]

Scherer's first application for a lectureship at the University of Vienna was blocked by Pfeiffer. Only the following year (1866) was he accepted as a *Privatdozent*, after Pfeiffer's objections had been overruled by government intervention. Scherer was a successful teacher; his lectures quickly gained popularity. After Pfeiffer's

---

[4] Bernhard Erdmannsdoerffer, "Alfred Boretius," *Preussische Jahrbücher,* CIV (1901), 5–6.

[5] *Goethe-Jahrbuch,* IX (1888), 250.

[6] "Nicht um dem obengenannten Buche eine Auszeichnung widerfahren zu lassen, die ihm in keiner Weise zukommt, sondern weil sie, nur in der einstimmigen Verurteilung des in den Zuthaten Müllenhoffs herrschenden rohen pöbelhaften Tones zusammentreffend, sich gegenseitig ergänzen, theile ich die beiden mir zukommenden Anzeigen hier mit. . . . Nicht unterlassen kann ich jedoch, hier schon den unwürdigen Ton zu rügen, womit Einer, der mit all seinem antiquarischen Kram dem grossen Mann nicht bis ans Knie reicht, an Jacob Grimm herumnergelt und sich seiner Bemerkungen als Ausganspunkt für alberne Spässe bedient. Für den aufmerksamen Beobachter liegt in diesem Verfahren allerdings nichts Auffallendes: es ist doch nur eine unverhüllte Fortsetzung dessen, was man im Stillen schon lange gegen den Mann geübt, dessen immer sichtbarer hervortretende Abneigung gegen Lachmansche Kritik unbequem zu werden begann." (*Germania, Vierteljahresschrift für deutsche Alterthumskunde,* IX [1864], 55).

death in 1868 the last obstacle to his promotion was removed, and during the same year the 27-year-old Scherer became a professor for "German language and literature" at the University of Vienna.

The main fruit of Scherer's Vienna years is his book *Zur Geschichte der deutschen Sprache* (Berlin, 1868).[7] While in the main a grammatical work, its preface contains a youthfully revolutionary program advocating the extensive use of linguistic and historical analogies. He calls for an uncompromisingly causative view of linguistic development and points to an intimate and necessary connection between linguistic laws and national character. The book created a great stir in professional circles; it had supporters as well as enemies and could not be ignored. Those who had become accustomed to Jacob Grimm's new advances in *Germanistik* and were somewhat rigid in their unqualified acceptance, suddenly found their doctrine put in doubt and endangered.

With the outbreak of the Franco-Prussian war of 1871, Scherer's position in Vienna became extremely difficult. He had never tried to hide his fervent pro-Prussian sentiments and hence was glad to heed a call to a newly founded German university in Strasbourg. It is likely that his *Geschichte des Elsasses von den ältesten Zeiten bis zur Gegenwart* (Berlin, 1871), which he wrote with his friend Ottokar Lorenz, was instrumental in gaining for him the support of the Strasbourg faculty.

The years at Strasbourg were happy and fruitful ones. Scherer revised a number of essays and lectures dating back as far as 1864. Together with some new material they were published in a book of an essentially non-technical character: *Vorträge und Aufsätze zur Geschichte des geistigen Lebens in Deutschland und Oesterreich* (Berlin, 1874).[8] In 1874 he and Ten Brink founded the periodical *Quellen und Forschungen zur Sprach- und Litteraturgeschichte*,[9] to which Scherer as well as outstanding seminar students contributed. After Scherer's death the journal was under the editorship of such distinguished scholars as Erich Schmidt (who had been one of Scherer's students and early contributors) and Andreas Heusler. In 1917 it ceased publication.

Scherer's concern during his Strasbourg years was increasingly with literary history rather than historical grammar, to which he

---

[7] Hereafter cited as *Geschichte d. d. Sprache.*
[8] Hereafter cited as *Vorträge und Aufsätze.*
[9] Hereafter cited as *Quellen und Forschungen.*

had hitherto devoted his best efforts. Out of his new inclination grew such studies as "Geschichte der deutschen Dichtung im XI. und XII. Jahrhundert" [10] and "Die Anfänge des deutschen Prosaromans und Jörg Wickram von Colmar. Eine Kritik." [11]

In 1877 Scherer received the coveted call from the Berlin University, which his old friend Müllenhoff had helped him obtain. The chair in Berlin, which had been especially created for Scherer, expressly included modern German literature, though even with this novel designation, no one more recent than Goethe was seriously considered suitable for academic study. Scherer's great verbal power and elegance as well as his rising fame made his lecture hall a Mecca for young students of literature. Wilhelm Dilthey attests to his infectious enthusiasm as a speaker.[12] After the publication of his literary history, honors were heaped upon him. He became vice-president of the Goethe society. He was present at the ceremony in Weimar (1885) which signaled the opening of the Goethe archives to scholars. He became advisor to the Grand Duchess Sophie for the preparation of the great Weimar edition of Goethe's works.

During the winter of 1884–85 he began to prepare lectures for a seminar on poetics (which he gave during the summer of 1885) and subsequently to expand and prepare them for publication. In many respects Scherer's *Poetik* represents the sum total of his theory of literature, which is remarkable for its opposition to abstract poetic concepts and its total negation of the validity of metaphysical penetration. It was an attempt to found a poetics on purely empirical principles, borrowed and adapted from the natural sciences. Impressed by the joy which Scherer derived from his last task, Dilthey wrote: "Never before had I seen him work with such cheerfulness and confidence." [13] During the winter of 1885–86, however, Scherer became ill and could no longer give his full energy to the work, and when he succumbed to a heart attack on August 6, 1886, the *Poetik* was left unfinished. The task of converting the lectures into chapters suitable for a book fell upon Scherer's student, Richard M. Meyer.

Whether or not Scherer's political inclinations led him to embrace

---

[10] *Ibid.*, VII (1874).

[11] *Ibid.*, XXI (1877).

[12] "Wilhelm Scherer zum persönlichen Gedächtnis," *Deutsche Rundschau,* XLIX–L (1866), 145.

[13] *Ibid.*, p. 144.

views on literary theory which were so much more at home in the Prussia of the late nineteenth century than in Austria, is a question which will probably remain speculative. It cannot be denied, however, that Scherer's fervent support of Prussian political causes went hand in hand with his admiration for those historians and literary theorists who emphasized the homogeneity of a specifically German spirit. He frequently expressed his distaste for what he considered the predominant Austrian spirit. In a newspaper article which appeared while he was spending his last year at the University of Vienna, he angrily attacked political conditions in his country, which were like an unfinished experiment by means of which history wishes to demonstrate the consequences of egoism.[14]

He rebelled against the spirit of reaction which had pervaded Austrian public life since the days of Metternich. He disliked the unquestioning subservience to the royal house and the domination of the Catholic church. To him the latter represented a powerful obstacle to intellectual progress, particularly since he held that such progress could be achieved only by the methods of natural science. Religion was to be relegated to the status of myth and superstition.

Scherer's aversion to the Austrian political and intellectual climate is evident in his essay on the dramatist Grillparzer, written soon after the latter's death in 1872. In the introductory remarks he writes, "I never liked Grillparzer," but then proceeds to justify his decision to study his works by the fact that the waves of enthusiasm for Grillparzer ran high in Vienna.[15] He comes to the conclusion— which we may well share—that Grillparzer was a master of stage technique, that his dramas, however, suffer from an attitude of resignation, a trait which Scherer attributes in turn to the political atmosphere of Austria. Scherer deals a harsh blow to the Viennese public when he discusses the dismal failure of *Weh' dem der lügt* in the *Burgtheater*. After expressing his dislike for the comedy on

---

[14] "Der oesterreichische Staat, in welchem alle centrifugalen Kräfte sich Stelldichein gegeben haben, worin die nackte Selbstsucht eines aufgeblasenen Natiönchens soeben noch dem unerhörtesten Triumphe nah war—der oesterreichische Staat steht da wie ein noch im Vollzuge befindliches Experiment, wodurch das Weltschicksal die Folgen des Egoismus und die Notwendigkeit des Gemeingeistes demonstrieren will. Wir aber schliessen die Augen vor den offenliegenden Tatsachen und rufen andächtig: o heiliger Mercurius, bitte für uns." (*Deutsche Zeitung* [January 12, 1872].)

[15] "Die Wogen der Begeisterung gingen in Wien endlich so hoch, dass ich es für meine Pflicht hielt, mich davon tragen zu lassen." (*Vorträge und Aufsätze*, p. 194).

surprisingly Aristotelian grounds—he does not believe that a mere kitchen boy lends himself to heroic treatment—he proceeds to castigate the audience of the première:

> But simply to hiss a poet like Grillparzer, to cast aside all respect for genius and to place the play, though it may be a failure, on a level with the arrogant experiments of hacks . . . that was tactless, uncharitable and above all cruel and will adhere forever as a flaw to the "gemütliche" Viennese public of the thirties.[16]

It is interesting that Scherer should have used this occasion for a condemnation of the Viennese public. He shared, after all, to some extent, the public's dislike for the play and it seems reasonable to conclude that Scherer's slap at the audience arose less from a desire to safeguard Grillparzer's stature as a dramatist than from pique at his compatriots.

Based on his observation that the Austrian state was one in which the bourgeoisie is excluded from the political life of the state, where the ordinary citizen can do nothing but "pray, earn a living and develop domestic and personal virtues," [17] he makes the hazardous claim that the character as well as the literature of such a state will necessarily take on certain distinctive features of meekness and domesticity. "No solid, forthright virility can thrive in these circumstances, and literature which arises out of such circumstances has at all times indulged in the glorification of domestic virtues and quiet serenity and has condemned all higher yearnings as empty ambition and intolerable presumption." [18]

Thus Scherer confidently establishes the direct relationship between social phenomena and imaginative writing by regarding the latter as the ineluctable result of the former. Conversely, he considered Grillparzer to have been at his best when he became articulate concerning his debt to German poets and German literature in general. He felt that whenever Grillparzer freely acknowledged his debt to Goethe—as he did on several occasions—this fact alone overshadowed his shortcomings. To Scherer, a love for Goethe automatically implied a love for the German spirit. By way of introducing a poem by Grillparzer dedicated to the memory of

---

[16] *Ibid.*, p. 304.
[17] *Ibid.*, p. 300.
[18] *Ibid.*

Goethe, he writes: "And yet there was a point where Grillparzer felt enthusiastically as a German." [19]

In matters of religion Scherer proceeds in an even more sweeping manner. Supported by his fervent belief in scientific causation, he concludes that all religious dogma is based on superstition, and by extending this notion he is led to the assertion that organized religion in Germany was at all times detrimental to literary creativity. In an essay entitled "Litteratur und Kirche" he builds his argument around the thesis that "The noblest creations stem from a spirit which stands partly in open, partly in secret opposition to the spirit of the church." [20] In order to prove such a contention, he adduces Walther von der Vogelweide, Wolfram von Eschenbach, and Gottfried von Strassburg as examples of German poets whose greatness resided in their emancipation from the spirit of the church. Three poets would seem to be insufficient to prove or even to buttress Scherer's argument, no matter how great their importance to German literature. Furthermore, to characterize all three of them as secret or overt opponents of the church certainly goes beyond mere oversimplification. But even if it were granted that much German literature displayed a certain independence from the prevailing dogma, it is still quite another matter to imply that such an attitude was the prerequisite, the *sine qua non*, for greatness. Yet this is clearly what Scherer means when he writes, "Because all greatness in the life of the spirit rests on independence and freedom, many of man's great spiritual accomplishments emerged in opposition to the church." [21] It clearly did not disturb Scherer to judge works of literature by his own moral and political standards, which while providing a note of vigor, honesty, and courage to his expressed views, at the same time severely limited his scope as a literary critic.

It should be noted that the discipline of philology in which Scherer had been trained, had departed from its sole preoccupation with ancient literary texts and expanded its field to include all the arts, religion, politics, and social studies. Philip August Boeckh, in

---

[19] The poem in question was one which Grillparzer had inscribed in a copy of *Der Traum ein Leben* to be sent to Weimar:

> So willst Du dahin Dich begeben,
> Wo Goethes Spur verwittert kaum?
> In Weimar war die Kunst ein Leben,
> Uns ist sie höchstens noch ein Traum.

[20] *Kleine Schriften*, I, 668.
[21] *Ibid.*, p. 672.

his influential encyclopedia of philological studies,[22] denied that philology should restrict itself to a study of ancient records from the point of view of linguistics. Instead it was to be a total national science encompassing the disciplines of linguistics, criticism, universal history, and many others. Boeckh had accepted one of the major principles of Giambattista Vico's *Scienza Nuova* (1725) and proposed the "impossible" goal of a universal "science of the known." [23]

In the course of some laudatory remarks concerning Carl Theodor Reiffenstein's biographical studies,[24] Scherer saw no departure on the part of the author from the legitimate preoccupation of philology when he attempted to reconstruct, among other minute details, the kind of view Goethe enjoyed from a particular window of his childhood home in Frankfurt into the neighboring gardens. It is difficult to determine just at what point, in Scherer's view, philological research begins to have relevance to a particular literary problem. Commenting further on Reiffenstein's studies, he concedes that his minutely biographical research had added nothing to a literary estimate of Goethe. However, he does not seriously object to it. Rather, this "striving for the genuine, original, authentic" is commended as "a kind of sport" which befits the philologist.[25] The task of finding the connecting links between extra-literary facts and the data inherent in the literary work appears to be assigned to a kind of intuitive vision which is self-evident and in no need of scrutiny. The discovery of such causative sequences, according to Scherer, is the supreme task of the literary historian. Accordingly the accumulation of facts borrowed from the provinces of other disciplines often assumes greater importance than the literary work under investigation. Once the spade-work has been accomplished, the literary critic or historian, it seems, has but to choose from the repository of facts to develop his hypothetical constructs. The questions of literary genre, style, and conventions

---

22 *Enzyklopädie und Methodologie der philologischen Wissenschaften* (Leipzig, 1877). Compiled and edited by Ernst Bratuschek from lecture notes dating back to 1809.

23 *Ibid.*, p. 15. Cf. Also pp. 11, 13 ff. For a more detailed account of the relationship between literary history and philology, see Julius Petersen, "Literaturgeschichte und Philologie," *Germanisch-Romanische Monatsschrift*, V (1913), 625–40.

24 Later collected in *Bilder zu Goethes Dichtung and Wahrheit* (Frankfurt, 1893).

25 *Aufsätze über Goethe* (Berlin, 1886), p. 21—herafter cited as *Aufsätze über Goethe.*

are treated as if they were of secondary importance. Only the "scientific" laws behind them are considered to be of true significance.

The best-known result of Scherer's scientific determinism is his postulate of a 300-year periodicity in German literature. According to this scheme, the most recent high point in German literary development is to be placed about the year 1800. German classicism is regarded as the culmination of a development which had begun immediately after the Thirty-Year War, and was still running its course during Scherer's lifetime. Presumably the period which began in 1650 would be completed approximately by 1950. The period of great Middle High German literature lasted from 1050 to 1350, and hence the three centuries between 1350 and 1650, the centuries of "Wyclif, Hus, the great Councils, Luther and religious wars" [26] by necessity constituted a period undistinguished in literature. In order to reach back to another time span of great literary significance, it is necessary to leap over the three centuries between 750 and 1050 A.D., which Scherer in his zest for the discovery of analogies, found in many respects similar to the "non-literary" period between 1350 and 1650. Both periods were concerned with religious dogma; and the writing was above all propagandistic.

> The entire epoch of three hundred years, from the middle of the eighth to the middle of the eleventh century, is comparable to the . . . period between 1350 and 1650. . . . The Carolingians, like Luther and the translators and printers before him, wanted to popularize the bible . . . a journalistic trend dominated poetry, as it dominated the religious pamphlets in Luther's time.[27]

By mathematical extrapolation, the earliest flowering of Germanic literature would then have to be placed around the year A.D. 600, a time during which, according to Scherer, the "national epos" was at its height, though he can cite only *Beowulf* (now dated about A.D. 800) as evidence for the latter claim.[28] Scherer further noted that the periods of greatness in literature invariably are accompanied by a quiet, unobtrusive dominance of women, and conversely, whenever women merely echo the deeds and thoughts of their men

---

[26] *Quellen und Forschungen*, XII (1875), 3.
[27] *Ibid.*, pp. 3-4.
[28] See Scherer, *Geschichte der deutschen Litteratur* (Berlin, 1883), p. 19—hereafter cited as *Geschichte d. d. Litt.*

and are relegated to a status of servility, all tender feelings disappear, the sense for delicate form—in life as well as in poetry—is lost.[29]

Scherer's sweeping theory of periodicity cannot be dismissed as a casual notion. It is, on the contrary, part and parcel of his life's work. After first noting a periodic alternation of male and female dominance in history,[30] he later expanded it into a full-fledged scientific hypothesis, designed—in true positivistic fashion—not only as an illumination of the past, but also as a guide to the future. The theory appeared essentially unchanged, on at least three separate occasions,[31] and was maintained in the face of rejection and even ridicule.[32]

Scherer was by no means the first to view literary history as a cyclic movement. Because of the striking similarities between Comte's and Scherer's overall views, it is possible to see the source of Scherer's cycles in Comte's law of three successive stages of knowledge, propounded in 1830 in the *Cours de Philosophie Positive*.[33]

An important impetus for such theories in nineteenth-century France stems from Jules Michelet's translation (1827) of Vico's *Scienza Nuova* (1725). It took a century for Vico's revolutionary historicism to make itself felt in Europe, and it had no direct influence on similar romantic views in Germany which had their source in Herder.[34]

A grand theory dealing with necessarily recurring literary peaks arises naturally from Scherer's methods, which he employed in other contexts on a minor scale. It involves the building of an all-encompassing perspective out of a variety of materials by means of the inductive technique borrowed from the natural sciences.

---

[29] See *Kleine Schriften*, I, 674.

[30] See *Preussische Jahrbücher*, XXI (1873), 493.

[31] *Quellen und Forschungen*, XXI (1873), 393; *Kleine Schriften*, I, 674; *Kleine Schriften*, I, 674; *Geschichte d. d. Litt.*, pp. 18–19.

[32] "Ich habe von den Feinden nur Spott, von den Freunden keine entschiedene Zustimmung geerntet." (*Kleine Schriften*, I, 675).

[33] E.g., Comte's introduction to the first *Cours*: ". . . chaque branche de nos connaissances, passe successivement par trois états théoriques différents: l'état théologique, ou fictif; l'état métaphysique, ou l'abstrait; l'état scientifique, ou positif" (5th ed. [Paris, 1892], I, 3).

[34] The influence of Vico's *Scienza Nuova* in France was traced from Michelet through Condorcet, Saint Simon, and Comte by George Boas in *French Philosophies of the Romantic Period* (Baltimore, 1925), pp. 265 ff.

Predictability is always a necessary adjunct. In 1879 he writes confidently: "I believe the alternation of masculine and feminine epochs to be capable of the widest generalization; it should be used deductively as a guiding principle based on the nature of heredity and sex."[35]

Clearly the stratum of literature proper is far too narrow for Scherer's endeavors. To him an insight into literature is not an end in itself, but is meant to serve as a stepping stone for the discovery of general sociological laws. One of the important methods which he used and whose further refinement he advocated is that of "reciprocal illumination" (*wechselseitige Erhellung*), a device which he first developed as a tool for the elucidation of linguistic phenomena. It is based on the premise that fundamental human activities are analogous and comparable in all periods of history. It is therefore possible to draw conclusions about a remote age of which we have only fragmentary records by applying to it the knowledge derived from our more intimate acquaintance with a modern period.[36] Applied to linguistics, this would mean that it is possible and indeed advisable to transfer the phenomena of the second German sound shift, which took place between the sixth and eighth centuries A.D., to the first or "Germanic" sound shift, which occurred in the course of the sixth and fifth centuries B.C. Conversely it would be equally fruitful, Scherer argues, to apply our knowledge of older occurrences to those of a more recent date and thereby enhance our understanding of the latter. Such arguments are quite in line with Scherer's positivistic conviction that similar causes will always produce analogous results. Indeed one might say that he is on fairly firm ground in the field of linguistics, so long as one accepts his premise that linguistic changes are explainable in physiological and biological terms. It will also be readily conceded that literary works of art are irrevocably tied to historical, environmental, and biographical factors, which are of great importance in that they

---

[35] *Kleine Schriften*, I, 657.

[36] "Überall trat der Begriff der historischen Gesetze in den Vordergrund. Wir verstehen darunter die Gleichförmigkeiten der menschlichen Lebenserscheinungen und verlangen ihre sorgfältige Beobachtung und Fixierung durch alle Räume und Zeiten hin. Wir hoffen durch die wechselseitige Beleuchtung vielleicht räumlich und zeitlich weit getrennter, aber wesensgleicher Begebenheiten und Vorgänge sowohl die grossen Processe der Völkergeschichte als auch die geistigen Wandlungen der Privatexistenzen aus dem bisherigen Dunkel unbegreiflicher Entwickelung mehr und mehr an die Tageshelle des offenen Spieles von Ursache und Wirkung erheben zu können." (*Geschichte d. d. Sprache*, p. 121).

provide a proper setting and perspective. To regard these factors as "causes" however and to elevate them to equal or greater importance than the work itself is to abandon the field of literary scholarship and to engage in studies more akin to philosophy of history and sociology. Also the direct causative relationship which Scherer confidently assumes to exist between vital experience and literary expression is certainly fallacious. His well-known formula, reminiscent of Taine's "race, milieu, moment," was first published in 1877, as far as I can determine. It calls for a precise analysis of "heritage, experience, learning" (*Ererbtes, Erlebtes, Erlerntes*): "[Goethe] developed this principle on a large scale and thereby prepared for us the road on which we now strive to advance step by step . . . as we seek to differentiate heritage from learning and experience . . . and try to discover the law which manifests itself therein." [37] By itself this does not indicate the extent to which Scherer is willing to reach beyond literature. In practice, however, his method has led to the kind of speculative recklessness which we observed in his theory of cycles.

Scherer was a supreme optimist with respect to the efficacy of the methods of the natural sciences and felt himself to be a member of a new generation in fundamental opposition to Hegel and his dialectical school. Thus he denied the value of a metaphysical interpretation of history (or literary history), which meant that the spirit of a work of art was not to be judged by any reference to pre-established aesthetic norms, but rather by relating it to the author and his intentions.

Hegel, who not long before had been hailed as the great master, was now the object of devastating attacks. The literary historian Hermann Hettner (1821–82) well exemplifies this drift away from Hegelian idealism toward materialism. Seven years after Hegel's death, Hettner moved to the University of Berlin and still held to the major tenets of Hegelian dialectic idealism. His dissertation (1843) was Hegelian, but with the essay *Gegen die spekulative Aesthetik* (1845) the turning point had been reached.

By "new generation" Scherer meant precisely those of his contemporaries who had overcome Hegel's teachings and accepted the positivistic theories which had come to Germany from France and England. His point of departure in the essay "Die neue Generation" (1870) is a collection of articles by Julian Schmidt from which he

---

[37] *Aufsätze über Goethe*, pp. 14–15.

singles out the statement, "The new generation is akin to the romantic school." With considerable rhetorical skill, Scherer begins by allowing for the possibility of such an analysis only to demolish it the more forcefully in the course of six polemical pages. He ends with a categorical rejection of speculative or idealistic systems and proclaims the natural sciences as the *signum temporis*. If one were to look for romantic residues, according to Scherer, they might be found in the "dynamic contacts of seemingly disparate branches of knowledge," but even here he demands more moderation than one could find among the romantics. The basis of modern *Germanistik* was to be the exploitation of source materials and of biographical details, for literature like all other intellectual disciplines, according to Scherer, is subject to the principles of the "determinacy of the will and of strict causality in the exploration of spiritual life."

Scherer's confidence in the all-encompassing power of the natural sciences was limitless. The following quotation, which represents the rhetorical high point of the essay "The New Generation," appears grotesquely naïve when viewed from the vantage point of our own age:

> The same power which brought to life railroads and telegraphs, the same power which called forth an unheard-of flowering of industry, increased the comforts of life, shortened wars, in a word, advanced man's dominion over nature by a colossal step—this same power also rules our intellectual lives: it makes a clean sweep of dogmas, it transforms the sciences, it puts its stamp on literature. Natural science triumphantly on its chariot of victory to which we are all shackled.[38]

Scherer readily acknowledged his debt to the apostles of positivism. He particularly admired the English thinkers and traced H. Thomas Buckle's materialism through Mill back to Auguste Comte.[39] However, he accepted the English materialist principles only in terms of their general application; he felt that German historians like Ranke had gone beyond the British. The German advance, according to Scherer, lay primarily in the discovery of

---

[38] *Vorträge und Aufsätze*, p. 411.

[39] "Die Hauptsätze der 'Physique Sociale' oder 'Sociologie' . . . sind in Mills Logik übergegangen und haben, zunächst wohl durch diese, auf Buckle gewirkt." (*Kleine Schriften*, I, 175.)

the "great harmonies of history" and of the "moments of great power and their regular recurrence at definite intervals." [40]

The use of analogy as a tool of literary and historical scholarship was felt by Scherer to have been a peculiarly German contribution. He singled out above all the economist-historian Roscher and the literary historian Gervinus,[41] who pointed the way toward the application of this method. He did, however, admire the second chapter of H. Thomas Buckle's *Civilization in England* (1843), which is headed "Influence exercised by physical laws over the organization of society and over the character of individuals." Part of this chapter deals with "imagination" as opposed to "understanding." Buckle contended that the former is produced in tropical, uncivilized countries, whereas "understanding" is peculiar to civilized countries blessed with a moderate climate. He took an altogether dim view of "imagination" and was totally unaffected by the creative attribute which his countryman Coleridge had given to it earlier. For Buckle it is superstition and religion which are invariably the concomitants of "imagination." Imagination "blinds the judgment" and ought to be curbed by an increase in "understanding." [42] Scherer, too, dismissed the notion of imagination as a creative power. For him it was essentially a process which reiterates experience, and can only be laid bare by a thorough and detailed investigation of the author's life. "The productions of the imagination are essentially reproductions." [43]

When Scherer called Buckle "one-sided" as compared to the German historians, he did not mean that his basic tenets were too limited, but rather that he had not included a sufficient number of environmental factors in his explanation of vital historical phenomena. Scherer asserted that Buckle failed to see the significance of political factors and that he neglected to account for the impact of geography on the intellect.[44]

A remarkable aspect of Scherer's hypotheses is the fact that they presuppose an implicit faith in a spiritual unity pervading the German-speaking regions through all recorded history. It is the spirit

---

[40] ". . . die Zeitpunkte höchster Kraftentfaltung und ihre regelmässige Wiederkehr in bestimmten Terminen." (*Ibid.*, I, 175).

[41] "Gervinus, der einzige Litterarhistoriker grossen Stils, den wir besassen." (*Ibid.*, I, 672).

[42] See Buckle, *Civilization in England*, 2 vols. (New York, 1858), I, 86 ff.

[43] "Bemerkungen über Goethes Stella," *Deutsche Rundschau*, X (1875), 78.

[44] See *Kleine Schriften*, I, 169.

of the nation as a whole which is at the center of Scherer's interest, and his positivistic theories paradoxically represent an attempt to penetrate to the origins of this intuitively perceived spirit. In the well-known dedication to his teacher Müllenhoff which precedes the text of *Geschichte der deutschen Sprache* he writes:

> The coming into being of our nation, seen from a particular vantage point, constitutes the main theme of this book. By means of physiological analysis and consistent characterization I have come to an explanation of the sound system of our language which led to the core of the unfragmented human personality, revealed moral impulses as an effective force and showed an unconditional, fervent dedication to ideal goals to be the mighty foundation which gave to our nation and language its first individual substance. Are you surprised when I confess to you that in all this there was something elevating for me?[45]

Scherer not only used historical relationships for his philological hypotheses, but also freely applied the evolutionary concepts which dominated the natural sciences since Darwin. Hence Scherer's tendency to value the growth and ultimate origin of a work of art even above the finished product. While he occasionally criticized specific aspects of the doctrines coming to him from the natural sciences, he apparently lacked the philosophical sophistication to set off his own views with any precision. In 1865 he writes: "Buckle's disquisitions concerning nature's influence upon the imagination and reason should be countered by a German by pointing to the eighth book of Herder's *Ideen*." [46] On the surface there seems to be ample reason for Scherer to regard Herder as one of his masters, together with Goethe and Justus Moeser. He frequently saw his own views supported by them. The "organistic" view of life involved as intimate a bond between the products of nature and those of the intellect as did the positivistic school, though the "organism" of the German classicists and romanticists was of a spiritual order; it had the dynamics of growth and development which were foreordained but not predictable.[47] Such a view always

---

[45] *Geschichte d. d. Sprache*, p. xiii.

[46] *Kleine Schriften*, I, 169–70.

[47] For an analysis of Kant's "organistic" view of literature, see René Wellek, "Aesthetics and Criticism," in *The Philosophy of Kant and Our Modern World*, ed. Charles W. Hendel (New York, 1957), pp. 65–89.

left room for the operation of an ultimate, irreducible power. Herder *compared* the literary work of art to life in nature, and usually the comparison was expressed in the form of a simile or metaphor from vegetable life; it was designed to throw light on literary facts for which an adequate vocabulary was lacking. Herder wrote: "What we know, we know only from analogy. . . . I run after images, resemblances, laws of congruence with the one, because I know of no other game for my thoughts. . . ."[48]

Scherer, on the other hand, *equated* the processes of nature and the creative mind and used the law of cause and effect to balance his equation. The result is a mechanistic view of literature which is crucially different from Herder's or Goethe's historicism. Where Herder urged empathy (*Einfühlung*), Scherer insisted on the documentation of peripheral or downright external facts. Both Herder and Scherer strove to arrive somehow at the authentic and initial poetic utterance of which the published version is only a more or less obscured extension. Herder attempted to reach his goal by a sympathetic submission to the author's spirit: ". . . for as the tree grows out of its root, so the progress and flowering of an art must be traceable to its origin which contains within itself the entire essence of its product, just as the complete plant with all its parts lies wrapped in the seed."[49]

It must be conceded that Scherer shared certain predilections with Herder as well as with romantic scholarship. (According to Scherer, Jacob Grimm represented the very peak of romantic scholarship.) Very important among these predilections was a concern with the origins of literature and language. Thus, in his desire to uncover the phantom of an "ur" form of poetry in general, or of specific poems like *Faust*, Scherer was quite justified in pointing to predecessors. Oskar Walzel went a long way toward defining the fundamental difference between the "organic" approach and the scientific one. For his analysis he availed himself of the concepts and terminology of the philosopher and "morphologic idealist" Hermann Friedmann,[50] whose key terms for the two mutually exclusive views are *Optik* and *Haptik*. In paraphrasing Friedmann's statements, Walzel writes: "He who perceives the world optically remains within the limits of morphological observation; he wishes to explain all being and becoming only by its configurations and

---

[48] Herder, *Sämtliche Werke*, ed. B. Suphan (Berlin, 1877–1913), VIII, 170.
[49] *Ibid.*, XXXII, 86.
[50] *Die Welt der Formen*, 2nd ed. (München, 1930), pp. 27 ff.

21

not to uncover binding laws upon which being and becoming depend." [51] Conversely, the goal of the "haptic" view is to find laws, and the establishment of a cause-and-effect structure is the primary object.

The approach of Herder, Goethe, and the romantics is "optic," and that of the natural sciences in the latter half of the nineteenth century is "haptic." Friedmann holds that it is a fallacy to assume that it is possible to comprehend a work of art by the "haptic" approach and illustrates his point by saying: "Trying to explain a perception of form—an optic impression—by means of an aggregate of substantive elements and their interacting forces—haptic impressions—is like trying to "grasp" a painting by reference to the dynamics of brush movements." [52]

The word "organic," more generally known than "optic" in this context, will serve equally well. An organic analogy enunciated by Herder or his followers, even when it is not metaphorical, is far removed from the kind of analogy which calls for the application of a scientific methodology. Literature as literature, rather than as a social document, is not responsive to the latter.

Very revealing of Scherer's position vis-à-vis romanticism is his full-length study concerning Jacob Grimm, which he wrote when he was only twenty-three, on the occasion of the death of the most revered German romantic scholar. Here Scherer in his first major study shows an astonishing skill and maturity in organizing large masses of material, and a kind of sympathetic insight which seems to indicate a warm relationship to German romantic scholarship. He consciously aimed at creating an overall intellectual picture of Jacob Grimm, and in this he was eminently successful. Intellectual and artistic trends are boldly characterized and evaluated as forces within a complex historical context. At this early stage he does not yet feel called upon to defend theories or even to subordinate intellectual currents to a causal scheme. While the subject of the study will alert us to Scherer's ties to German romanticism, we should not underestimate his youthful forays against the "unscientific" and intuitive procedures of his romantic predecessors. He attributed Grimm's involvement with fairy tales, mythology, and

[51] Oskar Walzel, "Wilhelm Scherer und seine Nachwelt," *Zeitschrift für deutsche Philologie*, LV (1930), 395.

[52] Hermann Friedmann, *op. cit.*, p. 31.

sagas to his romantic period, and the subsequent concentration on philology to his "defection from romanticism." [53]

Scherer pays some tribute to the devout concentration on detail evident in the early Grimm, combined with his superb gift for seeing hidden connections, but he expresses unstinting admiration only for Grimm's subsequent productive period beginning about 1825, which consisted of the "sublimation of his gifts by means of the scientific application of historicism to linguistics." Hence Grimm's monumental work, *Deutsche Grammatik*, whose four volumes appeared between 1819 and 1828, receives Scherer's highest accolade chiefly because it dealt the death blow to previous "speculative houses of cards" (*Kartenhäuser der Spekulation*). He correctly sees Grimm's *Grammatik* as the cornerstone of the discipline of *Germanistik*, yet he criticises as "romantic limitations" its strong antiquarian emphasis and its slighting of modern literary developments.

Scherer felt that romanticism's chief contribution had been its return to a national ethos as it revealed itself in history, language, and literature. He approved of its attacks upon French stylistic elegance and synthetic symmetries. The devaluation of French Aristotelianism had brought about a breakthrough to a literature truly expressive of its national character. On the other hand, Scherer had no use for somnambulistic creativity in romanticism, its traffic with the "night-side of nature."

In later works, Scherer's attacks upon romanticism became more explicit. Concessions to its methods and spirit become rare, and after the final accounting in the essay "The New Generation," can no longer be found.

Scherer's optimistic faith in the power of the new methodology leads him to discard all philosophic inhibitions with respect to its applicability to literary history. The all-important factual element (*das Thatsächliche*) is not further defined or qualified, but it is clear that the data intrinsic to literature, such as were named by Aristotle and elaborated in the Renaissance poetics, are excluded from this category. They are outside the province of the natural sciences and do not follow any known empirical laws. Empirical facts alone are to be sought as a valid basis for the supreme task of the literary historian or philologist, which is to select and ar-

---

[53] "Die Wendung zur Grammatik war sein Abfall von der Romantik" (Wilhelm Scherer, *Jakob Grimm* [Berlin, 1865], p. 88).

range such facts according to the law which brought them into being.

Scherer frequently reminds his readers that it is a scholar's duty to publish new philosophical insights as quickly as possible, even if they should prove untenable at a later date. He felt that their value lay in the stimulus which they would provide and in the energy which they would generate for the solution of recalcitrant problems. Sharing the optimistic faith of Grimm, he writes: " 'One must have the courage to err,' says Jacob Grimm, and hypotheses are necessary. That is still true today wherever new stimuli must be provided. Whoever has any to give, out with them!" [54] The suggestion is laudable and if followed could well bring fruitful ideas into the open which might otherwise be restricted to a small circle of professional colleagues. But his enthusiasm sometimes led Scherer to the promulgation of hastily conceived schemes lacking the marks of precise critical thought. It is not surprising that as a result he became the object of censure, even by his staunch friends. Julian Schmidt, one of Scherer's most fervent defenders, took note of his "deductive heat" and deplored the fact that his preconceived ideas often led him to a one-sided, or slanted, selection of facts. "But the selection of facts is too much determined by the eagerness of the deduction." [55]

Nor was Dilthey in any way persuaded that Scherer's method contributed to the advancement of philology, but he wished to pay tribute to a kind of intellectual heroism in the latter's struggle to find in literature general causal connections with the help of specific empirical facts:

> But while equipped with the results of all his devotion to exactness, and seeking to solve such universal questions as the inner causal nexus of our German literature or the formative principles underlying poetic structures, he could not eschew hypotheses, much as natural science cannot eschew them when faced with similar problems. . . . How he struggled here! [56]

Scherer's most prominent student, Erich Schmidt, though taking a positive view of the master's methods, shows an awareness of the risks involved in their employment. He speaks of Scherer's

---

[54] *Euphorion*, I (1894), 3.
[55] *Preussische Jahrbücher*, XXXV (1875), 316.
[56] Wilhelm Dilthey, *op. cit.*, p. 134.

"tumultuous boldness," which had led to hastily conceived and untenable intellectual constructs.[57] In 1879 Scherer had constructed a hypothetical ur-version in prose of Goethe's *Faust*,[58] and in 1887 Erich Schmidt made the well-known discovery of a copy of the actual *Urfaust* which proved Scherer's suppositions to be fallacious. Despite this, after Scherer's death Erich Schmidt writes modestly, though somewhat illogically: "The discovery of the *Urfaust* has cleared up some things and confused others, and I do not believe that merely as a result of this discovery Scherer would have had to give up the daring hypothesis of a prose novel. . . ."[59]

Despite setbacks, Scherer's partisans continued to adhere to his methods, a fact which becomes remarkable in the light of Scherer's last effort, the *Poetik*, which produced considerable consternation and put the Scherer school on the defensive. It must, no doubt, be taken into consideration that the volume, published posthumously in 1888, was put together and edited from lecture notes, student notebooks, and remembered conversations. The editor and Scherer's pupil, Richard M. Meyer, had frequently conversed with his teacher during the final months of his illness and reports in the introduction to the *Poetik* that during the preparation of this project Scherer had believed himself to have been at the height of his powers, that it was his expressed desire to see the notes published, and that he had appointed him, Meyer, to be the editor. Meyer asserts furthermore that by a thoughtful comparison of his three sources (Scherer's lecture notes, the "largely complete" notebooks of three members of the summer seminar of 1885, and his own conversations with Scherer) he was able to reconstruct the lectures "almost verbatim."[60] In addition, Erich Schmidt assisted with numerous suggestions in the preparation of the book.

It is therefore reasonable to assume that the *Poetik* does indeed represent Scherer's authentic thought arising directly from the notions which he had held, with minor variations, throughout his career. Yet Gustave Roethe feels that the *Poetik* fails to render fairly his teacher's thought, and dismisses the work by asserting that academic lectures pursue goals which are entirely different

---

[57] Erich Schmidt, "Wilhelm Scherer," *Goethe-Jahrbuch*, IX (1888), 259.

[58] Cf. "Der Faust in Prosa," *Aus Goethes Frühzeit* (Strassburg, 1879), pp. 76–93.

[59] Erich Schmidt, *op. cit.*, p. 259.

[60] See Wilhelm Scherer, *Poetik* (Berlin, 1888), pp. vi–vii—hereafter cited as *Poetik*.

from those of a book.[61] It is, of course, possible that for pedagogic reasons the tone and style of lectures differ greatly from that of scholarly articles or books. However, this should not prompt the reader to dismiss the lectures as unrepresentative.

Wilhelm Dilthey was less evasive. He had seen the lecture notes before they were published and was well acquainted with the development of Scherer's thought since the days of their close association in Berlin. He clearly stated his disagreement without attempting to question the authenticity of the then forthcoming book.

> While in former years, in the course of studies in literary history, we both confronted the question of whether the old problems of poetic theory might not be susceptible to a solution by the application of the tools of our time, it now became evident how far we had diverged from one another with respect to a method of resolution.[62]

The *Poetik* begins with an attempt to define the material with which literary scholarship should primarily concern itself. The following theorem, printed in italics, is the major conclusion of the first chapter: "Poetics is primarily the theory of verse; in addition, however, [it applies to] some instances of prose when it has a close relationship to verse." [63] It is difficult to think of a more superficial and mechanical division between poetry and non-poetry. One need not quarrel with the first statement because of the qualifying "primarily" (*vorzugsweise*); the second statement, however, is almost completely useless because Scherer does not make clear what he means by a "close relationship to verse." He excludes only one form of writing from the realm of poetics, namely a treatise in natural science written in prose, because it lays no claim to artistic effects and is not intent on stimulating the imagination.[64] A scientific treatise in verse, on the other hand, is *ipso facto* poetry, and Scherer takes Aristotle to task for specifically excluding didactic poems from the field of poetry, while including the Socratic dialogues. Scherer shows no hesitation in classifying all metrically structured language as poetry but is uncertain about the classification of prose.

---

[61] See Gustav Roethe, *Anzeiger für deutsches Altertum und deutsche Litteratur*, XXIV (1898), 242.

[62] Wilhelm Dilthey, *op. cit.*, p. 144.

[63] "Poetik ist vorzugsweise die Lehre von der gebundenen Rede; ausserdem aber von einigen Anwendungen der ungebundnen, welche mit den Anwendungen der gebundenen in näher Verwandtschaft steht." (*Poetik*, p. 32).

[64] *Ibid.*, p. 31.

It is here and only here that—according to Scherer—the distinctions become blurred. He notes with some alarm that a scientific treatise may well appeal to the imagination, while a novel may in no sense qualify as poetic material. It is apparent that he is unable to develop cogent principles for the choice of prose material that would belong to the province of poetry in the wider sense.[65]

Scherer then attempts to characterize and explain poetic modes by basing them on three ancient types of linguistic expression: choral song, proverbs, and fairy tales. The implication seems to be —though this is not made clear—that prose material which can be traced to one or several of these original types may be classed as genuine poetry.

Such an analysis is bound to be unsatisfactory, even impossible, if done with objectivity. The trouble stems from Scherer's original intention to avoid definitions, obviously because he is convinced that poetic principles are not definable from within and only partially from without: material written in verse is poetry because rhyme and meter can be determined by mechanical or "scientific" methods. A prose narrative cannot be classified as easily. It is poetic whenever it has "a close relationship to verse." Such a conclusion seems inevitable when we consider Scherer's aim as expressed in the introduction: "I am not greatly interested in grasping the essence of things by means of definitions, or to press [matters] into definitions. I'd rather refrain from devising definitions because so much nonsense has been perpetrated along these lines." [66]

The *Poetik* is indeed the final consequence of Scherer's factualistic empiricism. Because he denies the validity of inherently literary or aesthetic standards, he finds himself incapable of distinguishing good from bad literature or even literature from non-literature. In practice, of course, he overcomes this theoretical deadlock by means of intuitive evaluation or simple good taste. This theoretical impasse could not be better demonstrated than by his failure to recognize the Socratic dialogues as poetry as Aristotle had done. The extremity of his position makes it necessary for him to regard Aristotle as too prescriptive and not sufficiently impartial: ". . . Aristotle to me . . . is not sufficiently a natural scientist.

---

[65] As an afterthought Scherer modifies his view regarding poems dealing with natural science. He says that in order to qualify as poetry they must "of course not contain investigation but rather *representation* of the discovery." (Italics mine.)

[66] *Poetik*, p. xii.

For me he does not treat . . . the available literature with the cool observation and analysis . . . of a natural scientist. He is too much the legislator. He searches for the genuine tragedy and the genuine epos; he makes value judgments which are distinctly debatable." [67]

Value judgment in literature would therefore be a futile undertaking, and a sure guide to poetic value may be secured only by a study of the history of the effect on the public of a particular work:

> In the analysis of effects value judgments are indeed given. A kind of literature of which it can be said that it has affected the noblest human beings throughout history is certainly more valuable than another kind. But beyond that aesthetics need not go; it can refrain entirely from judgments of good and bad. [68]

It is significant that Scherer devotes almost half his *Poetik* to the relationship between the poet and his public and that he finds the development of poetic genres to be nothing but the poet's response to the desires of the public. This, of course, makes poetry subject to and indeed the slave of the laws of supply and demand. Indeed, Scherer holds that even in antiquity poetry was a type of merchandise to which the doctrines of economics could effectively be applied, and as a consequence he proceeds to use the concepts and vocabulary of economics, which he freely borrowed from the economist Wilhelm Roscher. [69] Such words as "exchange value," "merchandise," "production," "consumption," make their appearance, and it becomes clear that Scherer's view of literary value is, in a sense, democratic. Not only are literary values determined by the people, but the very act of literary creation is largely dependent on the author's sensitivity to what the public is likely to accept. Such well-established rules for a successful poetic production, as for example unity in variety, and probability, are not derived from the structure or meaning of poetry itself, but are to be considered aids in holding the public's attention and in producing suspense. Special sections of the *Poetik* are devoted to an analysis of audience reaction.

Of the major writers on aesthetics there is only Gustav Th.

---

[67] *Ibid.*, p. 43.

[68] *Ibid.*, p. 64.

[69] Cf. Wilhelm Roscher, *Kolonien, Kolonialpolitik und Auswanderung* (Leipzig, 1856). First appeared in *Archiv der politischen Ökonomie*, VI, VII (1847–48).

Fechner whom Scherer admires without major qualifications, and he quotes freely from his *Vorschule der Aesthetik* (1876). Scherer's dislike of Hegel's views has been mentioned, though he admits that Hegel occasionally had brilliant insights when dealing with individual literary phenomena. However, Scherer can do nothing with Hegel's disciple Fr. Th. Vischer, whose formalism appears to him even more rigorous—and hence more useless—than Hegel's. He commends H. Hettner's essay *Wider die spekulative Aesthetik*, but is disappointed that Hettner does not attempt to outline empirical aesthetics, but instead writes an art history. On the whole Scherer found far more support for his views among nineteenth-century philosophers of science (Darwin, Comte, Buckle), political economists (Roscher), and historians (Ranke), and men like Gervinus to whom literary history was a subsidiary branch of national history, than from men concerned exclusively with literature.

Dilthey felt that the crux of the difference between him and Scherer lay in the fact that Scherer underestimated the importance of psychology and had failed to include it as a factor in literary theory.[70] It is true that in developing "reciprocal illumination" and in his insistence on environmental causation, Scherer shows no great preoccupation with psychology. Both concepts, however, are unthinkable without a firm belief in the sameness and predictability of psychic reactions to known stimuli. But we need not content ourselves with mere assumptions, because Scherer was aware that psychology had to bridge the gap between extra-literary facts and literary phenomena proper. As early as 1866, in a review of a book on historiography, he insisted that the ultimate explanation of economic, geographic, and national influences must be sought in the field of psychology: "Classifications of phenomena and special descriptions of each particular class, species and kind will be the foundation of scholarship . . . the explanation . . . will in the end be pushed into the area of psychology in order there to seek the ultimate answer." [71]

In the *Poetik*, the work to which Dilthey's remark applies in particular, the large section dealing with the relationship between

---

[70] "Scherer verwarf jede Mitwirkung der Psychologie. Wie sich zur Zeit die vergleichende Sprachwissenschaft von der Benutzung psychologischer Sätze ganz frei gemacht hat, so gedachte er eine Poetik ganz mit denselben Hilfsmitteln und nach denselben Methoden herzustellen." (Wilhelm Dilthey, *op. cit.*, p. 144).

[71] *Kleine Schriften*, I, 171.

author and public is almost entirely psychological. In addition, there are scattered direct references to psychology throughout the book. Thus in speaking of the purifying effects of Homeric poetry, Scherer writes: "Here again one must reach for general psychological experience, for emotions which in part may be directly reproduced." [72]

He complains that Fr. Th. Vischer, whose Hegelian approach he dislikes, engaged too much in speculation and failed properly to take into account the principles of empirical psychology. [73] In a chapter entitled "Attention and Suspense," in which Scherer attempts to show how a poet might modify his work in order to attain the desired results on the public, he concludes his introductory paragraph: "It would be desirable to deduce the experiences available to us from the characteristics of human attentiveness which [in turn] must be delineated by psychology." [74]

It would seem then that here lies a basic misunderstanding on the part of Dilthey which he shares with the philologist Hermann Paul, who makes a supposed disregard for psychology an important factor in his altogether negative evaluation of Scherer. [75] Even though Erich Rothacker had pointed to this misunderstanding, [76] the erroneous impression has persisted that since Scherer was a positivist, he would have no truck with psychology. Thus Otto Wirth writes in a dissertation in 1937: "In harmony with these positivistic ideas Scherer rejected, for the sake of clarity and simplicity, the psychological approaches to literature." [77] While it is clear that Scherer's methods fell in line with those of the natural sciences of his day, it was not at all necessary to exclude psychology. In the early 1860's the economically oriented historian Roscher had written, "every science of natural life is psychological in nature," and Scherer specifically approved of this principle in 1866. [78]

It would be interesting to see to what extent and in what manner Scherer's literary judgments conform to his pronounced principles.

---

[72] *Poetik*, p. 68.

[73] *Ibid.*, p. 160.

[74] *Ibid.*, pp. 191–92.

[75] E.g., a passage in which Paul compares Scherer to Buckle: "Merkwürdig ist es, dass er wie Buckle absichtlich die psychologische Analyse verschmähte, und es liegt darin ein Hauptmangel seiner Behandlungsweise." (Hermann Paul, *Grundriss der Philologie*, 2nd ed. [Strassburg, 1901], I, 103).

[76] See Erich Rothacker, *op. cit.*, pp. 228 ff.

[77] Otto Wirth, *Wilhelm Scherer, Josef Nadler, and Wilhelm Dilthey as Literary Historians* (Dissertation, Chicago, 1937), p. 9.

[78] See *Kleine Schriften*, I, 171.

Even though he states that evaluation is unnecessary in the writing of literary history, his *Geschichte der Deutschen Litteratur* shows definite preferences and aversions. He gives those writers whose work tends to support his theory of cycles and who show some opposition to the prevalent church doctrines, more ample treatment than writers who would contradict his stated principles. He praises Luther's lyrical fervor and simplicity but has relatively little to say about Hans Sachs, indirectly justifying himself by writing: "With no other poet of the sixteenth century can the crudeness of an epoch be as tangibly demonstrated as with Hans Sachs." [79] While he felt an increasing kinship to Goethe, he maintained toward Schiller a rather cool respect. He curiously placed *Braut von Messina* highest among Schiller's dramas. His dependence on the "judgment of history" makes it necessary for him to end his book with Goethe's *Faust*, stating in a postscript that only thus can his history come to a worthy end. To deal with the most recent fifty years would be like a "confused and distracting appendix." [80]

It can be said that Scherer's evaluative criteria are sociological insofar as he used literary works as documents reflecting the vicissitudes of national life. An interesting case in point is his evaluation of Friederich Hölderlin. Not much can be said about his treatment of the poet in the *History*, except that he devoted only a single page to him in a work comprising 720 pages. The introductory remark, though purely impressionistic, is the most appreciative: "And unhappy Hölderlin who ended in madness sang some melodies which were so gripping that their tone still shakes us today." [81] Aside from the shortness of the treatment, the evaluation is moderately high, except for one sentence: "He preferred to revel in moods without form." [82] Much more revealing is an earlier article on Hölderlin which Scherer wrote in 1870. Amid high appreciation of individual poems he arrives at an essentially negative verdict. It must be said, however, that no one had as yet recognized Hölderlin's great stature as a poet. Not until Dilthey's critical essay, "Hölderlin," published in 1905, did his poetry receive any thorough critical attention, and a critical edition of his works appeared five years after the first World War.[83] Scherer builds his case on Goethe's

---

[79] *Geschichte d. d. Litt.*, p. 306.
[80] *Ibid.*, p. 645.
[81] *Ibid.*
[82] *Ibid.*
[83] Hölderlin, *Sämtliche Werke*, ed. N. v. Hellingrath, 2nd ed. (Berlin, 1923).

well-known negative judgment of Hölderlin. He points to the lack of sensuous elements in his poetry and objects to the Klopstock-like "amorphic idealism." [84]

These remarks, however, are only preparatory to the final argument, where Scherer's national ethos determines his criticism. He asserts that the basic feeling-tone pervading Hölderlin's entire poetry and life is one of despondency over the degradation of his fatherland. There is no acknowledgment whatsoever of the metaphysical passion inherent in Hölderlin's mature works. Instead he accuses him of having fallen victim to the "epidemic" of *Weltschmerz* which is anathema to Scherer and runs counter to his implicit faith in the all-embracing panacea of scientific progress. In fact he is so carried away by this idea that he uses the occasion to deliver a broadside against Schopenhauer, the great pessimist of his own century, and concludes by saying: "No, among us there is no longer any room for *Weltschmerz*. What business does Schopenhauer have with us? But also: what business does Hölderlin have with us?" [85] It would seem that Scherer's bias against metaphysics and pessimism is directed not only against philosophers and aestheticians but against poets as well. It is certainly far removed from the scientific objectivity which he often advocates. Poetry has become a vehicle for the expression of *Weltanschauung*. Scherer mistakes the particular bias of his own age for objectivity. For example, he belittles the Schlegel brothers because they came to the support of "astrology, magic, and all kinds of superstition." [86]

After Scherer had become settled in his post at the Berlin Academy, he occasionally dealt with contemporary literary works. In various journals and periodicals appear reviews of books by Gustav Freytag, Gottfried Keller, Berthold Auerbach. In a speech on Emanuel Geibel [87] he elevates this minor, though elegant, Munich poet to high importance in German literature. As a *Germanist* Scherer could not be expected to deal with Ibsen, Dostoievski, Tolstoy, and Zola, who had all written important works in his lifetime, but surprisingly he also failed to come to grips with such authors of real stature as Theodor Storm, Theodor Fontane, and Conrad Ferdinand Meyer.

---

[84] "Die gestaltlose Idealität Klopstocks hat sich in Hölderlin fortgesetzt." (*Geschichte des geistigen Lebens in Deutschland und Oesterreich* [Berlin, 1874], p. 351).

[85] *Ibid.*, p. 353.

[86] *Kleine Schriften*, I, 41.

[87] *Deutsche Rundschau*, XL (1884), 36–45.

Scherer's style in his book reviews is fluid and journalistic. His treatments are in the vein of appreciative essays rather than criticism. Gustav Freytag's *Soll and Haben* belonged to Scherer's formative experience, and he felt all the more an affectionate devotion to Freytag because he gave him the most endearing and imaginative picture of the Germanic past in the *Ahnen*.[88]

A review of Gottfried Keller's *Züricher Novellen* is most complimentary and contains only one mild reproach, which concerns the character Hadlaub.[89] In fact this review is refreshingly free from intrusions of theory. There is an easy flow in Scherer's language, an imaginative choice of metaphor, and an infectious, youthful enthusiasm. The anxiety with which Keller awaited the review of his work in the influential *Deutsche Rundschau* throws an interesting sidelight on Scherer's reputation. Keller understandably feared that the famous professor from Berlin would apply the standard of literal correctness to the character Hadlaub. In a letter of March 18, 1878, to his friend Julius Rodenberg, Keller wrote: "I await Professor Scherer's review with an anxious heart, since as an expert he will apply his cane especially on my Hadlaub, because of dissemination of false claims." [90] When the review finally did appear, highly favorable but for the expected reservation concerning Hadlaub, Keller remarked with a touch of humor: ". . . if only he had been as right everywhere as he was right about my Hadlaub." [91]

On the other hand, the name of Richard Wagner is anathema to Scherer. He ridicules him as a dramatist and composer whenever the opportunity arises, without giving a cogent reason for his attitude, although we may assume that it stems from his life-long aversion to "pessimism," to which he had objected in Hölderlin, Schopenhauer, and Grillparzer.[92]

The methods which Scherer had used effectively for literature up to the time of Goethe were patently inadequate when applied to contemporary works. His refusal to include books in his history dating back less than fifty years serves to confirm this conclusion. Scherer's chief merit lay in the enthusiasm for detailed textual and biographical research which he was able to instill among his students. His great stress on the importance of knowing the facts surround-

[88] Cf. Scherer's letter to Gustav Freytag, *Kleine Schriften*, II, 36–39.

[89] *Ibid.*, pp. 152–59.

[90] Emil Ermatinger, *Gottfried Kellers Leben*, 3rd and 4th ed. (Stuttgart, 1919), III, 237.

[91] *Ibid.*, p. 264.

[92] *Kleine Schriften*, I, 53, 718; also *Poetik*, p. 192.

ing and antedating the final version of a literary work of art encouraged the painstaking but invaluable work necessary for critical editions and detailed biographies. The mass of factual data was greatly enlarged and the tests for their reliability immeasurably strengthened. It included verification of dates, periods, and origins, as well as studies in correspondences between works of literature and concrete events.

The Scherer school lasted well into the twentieth century, although the impact of an important new movement was beginning to make inroads as early as 1890. Probably the last representative of the Scherer school was Edward Schröder, who died in 1942.[93] Alongside Scherer, but primarily after his death in 1886, Dilthey had elaborated a poetics which, like Scherer's, was avowedly empirical, historical, and scientific. Dilthey not only attempted to explore the link between external facts and literary expression, but the link itself was at the very center of his inquiry. Life and literature became a single psychic structure, and all critical efforts were bent on extracting the *Weltanschauung* of the author. Thus the very concept which Scherer had dismissed as irrelevant became fundamental to the new movement of the *Geistesgeschichte*.

---

[93] For an account of the history of the Scherer school, see Friedrich Bonn, *Ein Baustein zur Rehabilitierung der Schererschule* (Emsdetten, 1956).

BIBLIOGRAPHY

I. WORKS BY WILHELM SCHERER

Aus Goethes Frühzeit, mit Beiträgen von Jacob Minor, Posner, Erich Schmidt (Strassburg, 1879).

Aufsätze über Goethe (Berlin, 1886).

"Bemerkungen über Goethes Stella," *Deutsche Rundschau,* X (1875), 66–86.

"Emanuel Geibel," *Deutsche Rundschau,* XL (1884), 36–45.

"Geschichte der Deutschen Dichtung im elften und zwölften Jahrhundert," *Quellen und Forschungen,* XII (1875), 1–146.

Geschichte der deutschen Litteratur (Berlin, 1880-83).

Geschichte des Elsasses von den ältesten Zeiten bis zur Gegenwart, Ottokar Lorenz, collab. (Berlin, 1871).

Geschichte des geistigen Lebens in Deutschland und Oesterreich (Berlin, 1874).

"Jacob Grimm," *Preussische Jahrbücher,* XIV (1864), 632–680; XV (1865), 1–32; XVI (1865), 1–47, 99–139. Reprinted as a book under the same title (Berlin, 1865), rev. ed. (Berlin, 1885).

Kleine Schriften, ed. Konrad Burdach, 2 vols. (Berlin, 1893).

Poetik, ed. Richard M. Meyer (Berlin, 1888).

Rev. of Freytag's *Die Ahnen, Preussische Jahrbücher,* XXXI (1873), 481–502.

"Studien über Goethe," *Deutsche Rundschau,* XXXIX (1884), 240–55.

Vorträge und Aufsätze zur Geschichte des geistigen Lebens in Deutschland und Oesterreich (Berlin, 1874).

"Wissenschaftliche Pflichten," *Euphorion,* I (1894), 1–3.

Zur Geschichte der deutschen Sprache (Berlin, 1868).

II. SOURCES AND SECONDARY READINGS

Boas, George, *French Philosophies of the Romantic Period* (Baltimore, 1925).

35

Boeckh, Philip August, *Enzyklopaedie und Methodologie der philologischen Wissenschaften*, ed. Ernst Bratuschek (Leipzig, 1877).

Bonn, Friedrich, *Ein Baustein zur Rehabilitierung der Schererschule* (Emsdetten, 1956).

Buckle, H. Thomas, *Civilization in England* (New York, 1858).

Comte, Auguste, *Cours de Philosophie Positive*, 5th ed. (Paris, 1892).

Dilthey, Wilhelm, "Wilhelm Scherer zum persönlichen Gedächtnis," *Deutsche Rundschau*, XLIX (1886), 132–46.

Erdmannsdoerffer, Bernhard, "Alfred Boretius," *Preussische Jahrbücher*, CIV (1901), 1–22.

Ermatinger, Emil, *Gottfried Kellers Leben*, 3rd and 4th ed. (Stuttgart, 1919).

Fechner, Theodor, *Vorschule der Aesthetik*, 2nd ed. (Leipzig, 1898).

Friedmann, Hermann, *Die Welt der Formen*, 2nd ed. (München, 1930).

Gervinus, G.G., *Geschichte der poetischen National-literatur der Deutschen* (Leipzig, 1835).

——, *Grundzüge der Historik* (Leipzig, 1837).

Heinzel, Richard, *Kleine Schriften* (Heidelberg, 1907).

Herder, Johann Gottfried, *Sämtliche Werke*, ed. B. Suphan, completed by C. Redlich *et al.* (Berlin, 1877–1913).

Hölderlin, Friedrich, *Sämtliche Werke*, ed. Norbert v. Hellingrath, 2nd ed. (Berlin, 1923).

Körner, Josef, rev. of Scherer, *Geschichte der deutschen Literatur. Mit einem Anhang: die deutsche Literatur von Goethes Tod bis zur Gegenwart. Von Walzel, Literaturblatt für germanische und romanische Philologie*, XL (1919), 214–23.

Marholz, Werner, *Literargeschichte und Literarwissenschaft* (Berlin, 1923).

Müllenhoff, Karl, and Wilhelm Scherer (eds.), *Denkmäler deutscher Prosa und Poesie vom VII–XII Jahrhundert* (Berlin, 1864).

Paul, Hermann, *Grundriss der Philologie*, 2nd ed. (Strassburg, 1901).

Petersen, Julius, "Litteraturgeschichte als Wissenschaft," *Germanisch-Romanische Monatsschrift*, VI (1914), 150–51.

——, "Literaturgeschichte und Philologie," *Germanisch-Romanische Monatsschrift*, V (1913), 625–40.

Reiffenstenstein, Carl Theodor, *Bilder zu Goethes Dichtung und Wahrheit* (Frankfurt, 1893).

Roethe, Gustav, rev. of Scherer, *Kleine Schriften, Anzeiger für deutsches Altertum und deutsche Litteratur*, XXIV (1898), 225–42.

Roscher, Wilhelm, *Kolonien, Kolonialpolitik und Auswanderung* (Leipzig, 1856).

Rothaker, Erich, *Einleitung in die Geisteswissenschaften* (Tübingen, 1920).

Rychner, Max, *G.G. Gervinus* (Bern, 1922).

Schmidt, Erich, "Wilhelm Scherer," *Goethe-Jahrbuch*, IX (1888), 249–59.

Schmidt, Julian, *Geschichte der deutschen Nationallitteratur seit Lessings Tod* (Leipzig, 1866–67).

———, "Kritische Streifzüge," *Preussische Jahrbücher*, XXXV (1875), 313–22.

Schroeder, Edward, *Allgemeine deutsche Biographie*, XXXI (Leipzig, 1890), 104–14.

Troeltsch, Ernst, *Der Historismus und seine Probleme* (Tübingen, 1922).

Unger, Rudolf, *Aufsätze zur Prinzipienlehre der Literaturgeschichte* (Berlin, 1929), 1–32.

Vico, Giambattista, *Seconda Scienza Nuova*, ed. Benedetto Croce and G. Gentile (Bari, 1911–16).

Walzel, Oskar, *Wachstum und Wandel* (Berlin, 1956).

———, "Wilhelm Scherer und seine Nachwelt," *Ztsch. für deutsche Philologie*, LV (1930), 391–400.

Wellek, René, "Aesthetics and Criticism," *The Philosophy of Kant in Our Modern World*, ed. Charles W. Hendel (New York, 1957), 65–89.

———, *A History of Modern Criticism 1750–1950* (New Haven, 1965), IV, 297–303.

Wirth, Otto, *Wilhelm Scherer, Josef Nadler, and Wilhelm Dilthey as Literary Historians* (Dissertation, Chicago, 1937).

❧ Oskar Walzel ❧

THE APPEARANCE of both Scherer's and Walzel's names on the cover of the most widely read German literary history may well have created the impression that the two scholars held closely analogous views and that it was a feeling of intellectual kinship which impelled Walzel to undertake the task of bringing Scherer's work up to date. An examination of their writings should make it clear, however, that they differ widely and basically in methodology, philosophic premises, and indeed in *Weltanschauung*. The reason for Walzel's acceptance of the publisher's proposal to continue Scherer's *History* was practical rather than theoretical. It was a good business proposition for the new publisher, since in 1917 Scherer had been dead for thirty years and his work had entered the public domain; it was also an excellent opportunity for Walzel to be assured of a large public.

It should not be ignored that Walzel's academic training was almost exclusively in the hands of prominent men of the Scherer school: first Erich Schmidt and Richard Heinzel, and after Schmidt's appointment to the Goethe archive in Weimar in 1887, Jakob Minor as well. Walzel's alienation from Scherer's views was gradual and was probably delayed by the overpowering presence of his teachers; but it gained momentum with an increase in self-assurance and the stabilization of his position among literary scholars. The beginnings of those notions which led him finally to part company with naturalism and the positivist school of literary scholarship can be distinguished even in his very early publications. His ever-strengthening commitment to Catholic dogma and his early penchant for taking a "synthetic" rather than "analytic" view of literature must be re-

39

garded as important factors in Walzel's intellectual development.

Oskar Walzel was born in Vienna in 1864. His father was a prosperous grain merchant whose wealth and security were destroyed beyond repair in the market crash of 1875. It became necessary for Walzel's mother to gain a livelihood for the family. For the rest of his life Walzel admired the will power and tenacity of his mother. His first high school years were unimpressive scholastically; in fact he was required to repeat the fifth year. He received special instruction from a personal tutor, and it was only after the latter was dismissed that his record improved greatly. He felt himself on his own, and in a position to discover the importance of will power and persistence.[1] After taking his *Matura* in 1883 he immediately matriculated at the University of Vienna, and in 1887 took his *Rigorosum*, which he passed without particular distinction. By giving private lessons to high school students, he was able to save enough by the following year to travel north in order to attend lectures at the University of Berlin. With a doctor's degree in his pocket he could visit a variety of seminars without being obliged to follow a rigorous program. Thus he heard Treitschke, whose platform manner somehow frightened him. He was deeply impressed by Dilthey's lectures, and gratified to make his personal acquaintance, but was taken aback by Dilthey's remark that Friedrich Schlegel, great though he was, held no interest for him after his conversion to Catholicism.

It is curious that despite Walzel's obvious involvement in his chosen profession, it was not until ten years after his *Rigorosum* that he began to give lectures at a university. Soon after his return to Vienna from Berlin he became tutor to thirteen-year-old Leopold Andrian-Werburg, the son of a prominent Viennese family.[2] In the luxurious Andrian household he was treated as a member of the family. He travelled much and was engaged in what he liked to call *vita activa*, which included a sensational and tragic love affair with a once celebrated opera star, then in her sixties.

During a summer vacation in 1892, Walzel met the daughter of a banker and two years later married her. She appears to have been

---

[1] "Zum erstenmal in meinem Leben entdeckte ich, dass ich etwas wollen und durchsetzen könne." (*Wachstum und Wandel, Lebenserinnerungen von Oskar Walzel*, ed. Carl Enders [Berlin, 1956], p. 6—hereafter cited as *Wachstum und Wandel*).

[2] Baron Leopold Andrian became known as a minor poet and member of literary circle which included Hermann Bahr and Hofmannsthal. In 1918, he became manager of the *Wiener Hoftheater*.

largely responsible for leading Walzel to a *vita contemplativa*. Her Jewish background was fated to become the source of profound anxiety during the reign of Nazism in Germany. Her conversion to Catholicism before her marriage, of course in no way alleviated the problem.

In 1893, Walzel took a position as a librarian at the *Hofbibliothek* in Vienna, and used his considerable free time to prepare himself for his *Habilitation*, which would qualify him to lecture at a university. Because he had already published several scholarly articles, he was not required to submit a *Habilitationsschrift*, but instead was to be tested in a colloquium directed by Jakob Minor. Unsuccessful at first, he was required to take it again (1894). The following year he became *Privatdozent* at the University of Vienna, and in addition took on a literature class at a high school for girls.

In 1897 he submitted his credentials to the University of Bern, and was appointed to his first position as *Ordinarius*. He spent a fruitful ten years there and improved his lecturing technique to a point where his seminars became among the most popular in Bern. Although Walzel enjoyed his Swiss sojourn, he looked for an apportunity to obtain a position in Germany. Germany to him meant not only the intellectual center for German-speaking peoples, but it had become a political center of gravity as well, ever since the war of 1870–71. Bismarck's campaign in France had given Walzel the first deep impression of heroic effort on a large scale. Bismarck, Moltke, and the Crown Prince, whose pictures he had seen in newspapers, had been the great heroes of his childhood.[3]

The opportunity came in 1907, in the form of a vacancy at the Institute of Technology in Dresden, created by the death of the literary scholar, Adolf Stern. In order to increase his income, Walzel took on the additional task of giving lectures at the Academy of Fine Arts, a position which had once been held by Hermann Hettner. During the fourteen years at Dresden, Walzel became well known throughout Germany. He was called on to lecture in various German cities, and during the first World War, he went to friendly capitals as a German cultural emissary. After the immensely successful *Scherer-Walzel* had been published, his fame in Germany spread through ever widening circles.

In 1921, the University of Bonn extended an advantageous offer.

---

[3] "Zu Weihnachten 1870 wollte jeder Junge und auch ich eine Pickelhaube haben." (*Wachstum und Wandel*, p. 97).

Walzel yearned to lecture at a university rather than at an institute of technology, and it was also the prospect of far more free time for writing and research which made the Bonn offer attractive. He accepted, and never had cause to regret it. He received many honors, and was able to gather in the fruits of his labors. When the introductory volume to the sumptuous *Handbuch* series was published, the literary world had access to a comprehensive exposition of Walzel's theoretical position. In terms of influence and scholarly eminence, he had reached his peak. He was retired at the age of seventy in 1933, and his successor was Karl Justus Obenauer, who gave his introductory lecture dressed in Nazi uniform.[4] Walzel's generally pessimistic outlook on life received its final confirmation in 1944 in Bonn, when his 74-year-old, ailing wife was taken from his side by the Gestapo and transported to Theresienstadt in occupied Czechoslovakia, where she died a month later. In December of the same year, Walzel was killed in an Allied air raid. He was eighty years old.[5]

Beginning about 1905, Walzel produced an ever increasing number of essays, talks, book reviews, and books. Thus the development of Walzel's literary theory may be traced in some detail. By about 1910 certain important notions, which became the dominant preoccupations of his career, began to crystallize.[6]

The bulk of his ideas, however, is presented in his chief theoretical work, which he prepared as an introduction to a large set of volumes covering the major world literatures, *Handbuch der Literaturwissenschaft*, an ambitious undertaking of which he was the editor-in-chief. It is this introductory volume, called *Gehalt und Gestalt im Kunstwerk des Dichters* (1923) which will hold much of our attention in our interpretation of Walzel's views. There is

---

[4] Obenauer achieved notoriety in the famous exchange of open letters with Thomas Mann, in the course of which the latter's honorary doctorate was revoked.

[5] Most of the biographical information has been gleaned from Walzel's personal memoirs, which were uncovered among the ruins of his house. A few illuminating personal details, such as instances regarding Walzel's innate pessimism and social standoffishness, may be learned from an article written by his friend and professional colleague, Carl Enders, entitled "Oskar Walzels Persönlichkeit und Werk," *Zeitschrift für deutsche Philologie*, LXXV (1956), 186–99. The article, however, contains no evaluation of Walzel's work.

[6] A complete bibliography of Walzel's writings up to the year 1924 was prepared by one of Walzel's former Bern students, Edith Aulhorn, and appended to the *Festschrift für Oskar Walzel* (Wildpark-Potsdam, 1924).

no evidence that his theories underwent important changes after 1923.

Walzel's literary style has none of the journalistic zest and smooth elegance of a Scherer. His sentences move haltingly, often clumsily, and adhere rather too long to minutiae. His method is eclectic. Haltingly expressed opinions are interspersed in large masses of second-hand material even in a book like *Gehalt und Gestalt* which, one would expect, would be devoted primarily to Walzel's own theory. In contrast to Scherer's optimistic, exhortatory rhetoric which sweeps all obstacles aside, Walzel shows caution and hesitancy, a quality which his friend Julius Wahle called a "deeply piercing intellectuality" (*tiefbohrender Scharfsinn*).[7]

It will be well briefly to isolate those areas in literary scholarship which, more than others, preoccupied Walzel, before we proceed to a more detailed and critical examination. The compass of Walzel's concerns is far greater than Scherer's. His reading and critical judgments range over philosophy as well as literature. In addition to his learning in *Germanistik*, he showed respectable erudition in English and French literature; while his training was true to tradition, and concerned itself with literature of past generations, Walzel soon showed an intense interest in the post-Goethe period, and indeed in his own contemporaries.

In broadest terms, Walzel's life work was directed toward two fundamental goals: 1) to establish and solidify the autonomy of art in general and of literature in particular, and to free literary criticism from domination by non-aesthetic disciplines; 2) to develop broad, morphological categories for imaginative literature by the isolation of common or contrasting criteria, and to illuminate such categories by finding analagous structural aspects in the visual arts.

The two goals are by no means always separable; most often they imply one another, but generally speaking, it can be said that the attempt to isolate formal elements and to stress their importance was the primary concern of his early years. With the advent in 1915 of Wölfflin's book, *Kunstgeschichtliche Grundbegriffe*, he began to develop what he and others considered a full-fledged formalistic theory of literary criticism.

Walzel was by no means the first to oppose the positivist and materialist schools of literary history. Early, vehement attacks against

---

[7] Julius Wahle, in a letter to his friend Walzel on the occasion of his sixtieth birthday. (*Festschrift für Oskar Walzel, op. cit.,* p. 224).

positivism had been directed not so much against Scherer himself, but rather against his epigones, as for example Düntzer. Accusations in newspaper *feuilletons* included journalistic slogans picturesquely descriptive of what were considered obsessions of the Scherer school, such as hunting for "ur"-versions of literary works and for biographical minutiae.[8] Under the circumstances, H. Maync, in his *Rechtfertigung der Literaturwissenschaft* (1910) could effectively uphold Scherer's own methods by pointing out that the master himself would not have approved of his lesser disciples. Maync was able to call attention to Scherer's disdain for such extremist applications of his principles. (Scherer spoke of "micrology" and "coastal navigation.")

More telling attacks against the Scherer school came from the creative quarter. Such writers as Lilienkron, Dehmel, and Spitteler took adverse positions toward the "scientific" approach to literature. Peter Rosegger, for example, on the occasion of the discovery (1910) of the "Ur-Meister" wrote: "Heaven forbid that they should edit not only finished works but first jottings as well." [9] Such outcries by important literary men echoed throughout Germany. R. M. Meyer felt it incumbent upon him to lodge a vigorous protest against this trend.[10] He regarded the scholarship of the Scherer school, even including some of its amateurish excesses, as proper and adequate because it was solidly based on the operations of common sense.

Although Walzel was in a sense an unfaithful disciple of prominent men of the Scherer school—Minor, Schmidt, and Heinzel—he nevertheless stood by no means alone in his opposition to theoretical positivism and materialism; nor was his a lonely voice against naturalism and impressionism. He looked back with a sense of gratitude to the book by the sculptor Adolf v. Hildebrand, *Das Problem der Form in der bildenden Kunst* (1893), in which great emphasis was placed on the crucial difference between nature and art, which his contemporaries had neglected. During the high point of impressionism in the fine arts Hildebrand found it necessary to stress the importance of form, and he took steps to define it conceptually.

---

[8] "Gegenwartsfremdheit, Parallelenjägerei, Unterrockschnüffelei, Kadaver-seziererei." (See Oskar Benda, *Der gegenwärtig Stand der Literaturwissenschaft* [Wien, 1928], p. 8).

[9] Quoted from *ibid.*, p. 9.

[10] See "Philosophische Aphorismen," *Germanisch-Romanische Monatsschrift*, III (1911), 497–98.

Moreover, Walzel was able to point to one of his own students, Wilhelm Worringer, once a member of his seminar in Bern, who had gone far in defining contrasting pairs of aesthetic forms with respect to classic and Germanic, or gothic, ornamental designs.[11] Hildebrand and Worringer were particularly dear to Walzel because they were preoccupied with the formal element in art. Opposition to the Scherer school, however, far more influential than these isolated efforts, came from the movement later known as *Geistesgeschichte*. Indeed, positivism in literary history was not succeeded by Walzel's or anyone else's formalism, but by the sophisticated and philosophically well-grounded school which looked upon Wilhelm Dilthey as its founder. Walzel's estimate of the towering figure of Dilthey was very high indeed, and yet he avoided being completely identified with his methods.

Another source of opposition to the methods of the Scherer school came from Karl Vossler. While Walzel worked out his own theories independently of that scholar, he singled out for praise Vossler's article "The Relationship between the History of Language and the History of Literature," in which the methods of *Geistesgeschichte* are vigorously opposed.[12] While emphatically agreeing with the main thesis, Walzel felt that Vossler unduly limited himself by basing his literary analyses too exclusively on linguistic and grammatical categories.[13]

The domination of positivism over German literary scholarship had already been broken by the historically and psychologically oriented *Geistesgeschichte* which grew in strength in the wake of the overpowering figure of Wilhelm Dilthey; nevertheless it is misleading to say, as Oskar Benda does,[14] that Walzel merely engaged in shadow-boxing when he took a position against the positivist school in his *Gehalt und Gestalt*, on the grounds that it had been effectively repudiated about ten years earlier. As a matter of fact,

---

[11] See Worringer, *Abstraktion und Einfühlung* (München, 1908).

[12] E.g.: "Demgegenüber haben tiefer blickende Kunsthistoriker von jeher gesehen und verstanden, dass die Kunst nicht nur ein allseitig bedingtes Ergebnis der historischen Kulturen und der psychologischen Naturen, sondern auch eine durch sich selbst bedingte Tätigkeit ist, und dass sie als solche ihre eigenen Probleme und ihre autonome Spezialgeschichte hat." (Karl Vossler, *Gesammelte Aufsätze zur Sprachphilosophie* [München, 1923], p. 26).

[13] See *Gehalt und Gestalt im Kunstwerk des Dichters*, part of series: *Handbuch der Literaturwissenschaft*, ed. Oskar Walzel (Berlin, 1923), p. 31—hereafter cited as *Gehalt und Gestalt*.

[14] Oskar Benda, *op. cit.*, p. 8.

45

Walzel began to formulate his own views as early as 1909,[15] when he joined forces with Dilthey in the task of wresting art criticism from the grip of the natural sciences. He early recognized two components in Scherer's literary scholarship. One of these was romantic historicism, which he rightly regarded as anti-individualistic. During the same year, Walzel took note of the second major component of Scherer's methodology: Comtean positivism. He pointed to the common elements existing between the two components: the extinction of the individual as a significant factor, and the opposition to metaphysics. At the same time, however, Walzel showed an awareness of irreconcilable conflict between them. Comtean positivism did not recognize a "national spirit." The "organic" view of Herderian historicism which allowed for such a spirit was foreign to Comte and his followers. Scientific causation took the place of organic or inner necessity. Hence positivism was more interested in the *relationship* between historical phenomena than in their actual character. Walzel saw that the principles of scientific determinism had been adopted essentially unaltered by Scherer, and then merged with a romantic view of literary history. All in all, Walzel considered the marriage of historicism and positivism unsuccessful.

As early as 1910, Walzel saw in Dilthey's writings support for his own view that there was a great need to explore "the form" of a work of art and to treat it as an entity susceptible to conceptual analysis:

> Dilthey's hints point the way to the "synthetic" scholar. They adumbrate a requirement for all synthesis: the concept. Conceptual elements which go beyond a mere re-experiencing exist in history. A much greater number of conceptual elements are available to the literary scholar. I only single out the most important: the ideal which is realized by the work of art . . . the form through which it takes shape.[16]

Walzel freely acknowledged his debt to Dilthey in many publications, and yet the question which imposes itself is whether Dilthey's principles are not essentially foreign to the system which

---

[15] See Walzel's "Analytische und synthetische Literaturforschung," *Germanisch-Romanische Monatsschrift* (1910), pp. 257-74, 321-41, reprinted in *Das Wortkunstwerk* (Leipzig, 1926), pp. 3-35—the latter hereafter cited as *Wortkunstwerk*.

[16] *Ibid.*, p. 20.

Walzel tried to develop. He never openly disagreed with Dilthey, though it is clear that his formal and conceptual approach to criticism is not compatible with Dilthey's psychologism and historical relativism. While he professed to accept Dilthey's new concept of *Erlebnis*, he showed paradoxically strong anti-psychologistic leanings. He tried to make full use of Dilthey's famous "three types" [17] while elaborately denying that they were based on psychological differences in the artist's personality.

Dilthey's three types of *Weltanschauungen* are:

1. *Materialism* and *Positivism*, based on the natural sciences and represented by such men as Democritus, Lucretius, Hobbes, and Comte. The processes of nature and of the intellect are viewed as analogous. The only reality is physical nature, and the study of nature is the highest endeavor.

2. *Objective Idealism*, exemplified by Heraclitus, Spinoza, Leibniz, Shaftesbury, Goethe, Hegel. "Feeling" is at the core of this world view. In contrast to the first type, the meaning and purpose of existence, as well as moral values, are of crucial importance. God is seen as immanent in the manifestations of nature, and hence pantheism and panentheism are natural subdivisions of this type.

3. *Idealism of Freedom* (Plato, Corneille, Kant, Schiller, Carlyle). This type is characterized by the independence of the spirit from nature. The sovereign personality projects its concepts upon the universe.[18]

This grand division encompassing all thought and art constituted, according to Walzel, a purely philosophical scheme akin to Kant's *Kategorien*, as defined in paragraph XI of *Critique of Pure Reason*, in spite of Dilthey's insistence that the psychological concept of *Erlebnis* is at the center of all poetry.[19] Furthermore, he did not account for the fact that Dilthey's aesthetics is based on *Gefühlskreise*, which are introduced to elucidate form as well as content in psychological terms.[20]

Only occasionally does Walzel hint at differences between himself and Dilthey. He "dared to extend" Dilthey's philosophic categories,

---

[17] As elaborated in Dilthey, "Typen der Weltanschauung," *Gesammelte Schriften* (Berlin, 1923), VII, 100–12.

[18] For a detailed discussion of Dilthey's critical theories, see René Wellek, *History of Modern Criticism* (New Haven, 1965), IV, 320–25.

[19] Cf. Kurt Müller-Vollmer, *Towards a Phenomenological Theory Literature, A Study of Wilhelm Dilthey's Poetik* (The Hague, 1963), pp. 33–41.

[20] Cf. René Wellek, "Wilhelm Dilthey's Poetics and Literary Theory," *Festschrift für Hermann J. Weigand* (New Haven, 1957), pp. 127–32.

and, encouraged by the work of Herman Nohl, he wished to explore the problem of formal analysis by employing the tools developed by Dilthey, though such tools were concerned with spiritual content rather than form.[21] It should not be forgotten that it was also the Austrian philosopher Johann Friedrich Herbart who had convinced him of the basic necessity to posit both form and content in a work of art—as against the widespread German penchant for a consideration of content only. He was not remiss in expressing his debt.[22]

Walzel was constantly afraid of being called a "mere formalist." He often made a point of asserting that he had always regarded the "contents" of a work of art of great importance and that he had set himself the task of exploring its form only because it had hitherto been neglected. However, in *Gehalt und Gestalt* he states with considerable assurance that the need of his generation is for a code of criticism built on a modern epistemology. He writes:

> For the past two decades, the logicians have been defending themselves against the encroachments of scientific psychologists. The explorer of artistic creations must also struggle against a confusing psychologism. While I cannot be expected to push aesthetic creativity into the realm of logic, I still feel that those who wish to comprehend such creativity remain closer to the laws of the intellect, i.e., logic, than to a kind of soul analysis which employs the methods of natural science.[23]

He lauds Dilthey for having clarified and enriched the concept of *Gehalt*, but obliquely criticizes him for having neglected equally important problems of form. He wishes to move on to a field which would allow him to explore *Gestalt*.

Although Walzel expended much effort on a clarification of *Gestalt*, it still remained a vacillating concept, moving freely between the extremes of mechanical metrics on the one hand and

---

[21] "Um so wichtiger ist mir, an dieser entscheidenden Stelle zu zeigen, wie von Diltheys drei Typen weitergegangen werden kann in die Erschliessung des Wesentlichen künstlerischer Form. Ich wage es, an einer kleinen Reihe von Erscheinungen nachzuweisen, wie mit Diltheys Mitteln gegensätzliche Formmöglichkeiten sich erfassen lassen." (*Gehalt und Gestalt*, p. 86).

[22] "Herbart und seiner Nachfolger Verdienst ist, diese Scheidung von Form und Gestalt gefordert und im Gegensatz zur Aesthetik des deutschen Idealismus die Bedeutung dieser Scheidung nachgewiesen zu haben." (*Wortkunstwerk*, pp. 80–81).

[23] *Gehalt und Gestalt*, p. 9.

pure "content" on the other. His most concise definition appears to be the following: "Structure [*Gestalt*] in literature is everything that acts upon the inner and outer senses, that speaks to the ear or to the eye, or awakens visual images." [24] It is important to note that Walzel avoids the use of the word "form" in this definition, and indeed the title of his chief work, *Gehalt und Gestalt*, eschews the old form versus content controversy by resorting to the terminology of German classicism.[25] The increased comprehensiveness of the concept of *Gestalt*, however, was obtained at the expense of clarity. The plot or fable of a literary work of art—which Walzel surely would wish to be considered as *Gehalt*—may yet speak to the ear as well as to the eye, and therefore come under the heading of *Gestalt*. By making a distinction between external, formal elements, such as meter and rhythm, and an "inner form," Walzel compounds the difficulty. Whereas meter, rhythm, style are at least describable in conceptual terms, the absorption of "inner form" into Walzel's concept of *Gestalt* makes that term so broad as to impair its usefulness.

By 1915 Walzel had dealt exhaustively with the concept of inner form[26] and noted its appearance in Giordano Bruno's *Eroici Furori*, and a century later in the Earl of Shaftesbury's writings where Plotinus' *endon eidos* was first translated as "inward form," which was taken over by Herder, Goethe, and Wilhelm von Humboldt as *innere Form*. Walzel felt that Plotinus had achieved a great advance over Aristotle's *Poetics*, and largely accepted Plotinus' concept of inner form as his own. "This form," he writes, "does not depend upon technical devices but rather means the inner relationship between the outward appearance of the work of art and its spiritual matrix." [27] Plotinus' inner form and what might be called

---

[24] *Ibid.*, p. 178.

[25] The well-known section of Plotinus' *Enneads* (V, 8, 1) where an artfully carved stone is compared to one in its natural shape, contained the Greek *eidos* which Goethe translated as *Gestalt*. The translation was sent to Zelter on September 1, 1805, and only in 1829 incorporated in the appendix to *Wilhelm Meisters Wanderjahre*, known as "Makariens Archiv." Goethe wrote: "Euch wird aber der Stein, der durch die Kunst zur schönen Gestalt gebracht worden, alsobald schön erscheinen; doch nicht weil er Stein ist, denn sonst würde die andere Masse gleichfalls für schön gelten, sondern daher, dass er eine Gestalt hat, welche die Kunst ihm erteilte." (*Goethes Sämtliche Werke.* Jubiläumsausgabe in 40 Bänden [Stuttgart, 1902-7,] XXXV, 316).

[26] *Vom Geistesleben alter und neuer Zeit* (Leipzig, 1922), pp. 1-57—hereafter cited as *Geistesleben*.

[27] *Ibid.*, p. 33.

"outer form," such as rhythm, meter, etc., would seem to be irrevocably interrelated and may be considered to constitute the total concept of *Gestalt*.[28]

It is clear that with such a great expansion of the concept of form, the place of "content" in a literary work of art becomes rather precarious. Yet Walzel insists on maintaining the distinction and produces a concise definition of *Gehalt*: "I count as content [*Gehalt*] all aspects of recognition, volition, feeling contained within or caused by the literary work of art." [29] It requires no great effort to see that the two definitions are bound to show areas of overlap and tautology. The "recognition," "volition," "feeling" of the above definition could easily be substituted for "everything that acts upon the inner and outer senses" in the definition of *Gestalt*.

Walzel tried hard to introduce a clear division between form and content, yet constantly bogged down in considerations which show the inseparability of the two. It cannot be denied, certainly, that he was justified in feeling that German literary scholarship had been preeminently preoccupied with questions of philosophic and ethical content and that there was a great need to create an awareness of the structural aspects of literary works. At least partially he fulfilled this need. On the other hand, he seriously impeded his contribution by attributing vague and sometimes contradictory qualities to his concept of form, which appears at times to be related to neo-platonic ideas and at times to rhetorical categories.

The term "higher mathematics" is introduced (as contrasted to a mere analysis of metrics which is "lower mathematics") and defined as the exploration of the relationship between *Gehalt* and *Gestalt*. "Higher mathematics" should be capable of unraveling the grand design pervading the literary work of art. In applying it to poetry, Walzel leans heavily on August Wilhelm Schlegel, describing in detail his speculations on the ethical significance of certain verse forms. He is particularly impressed by Schlegel's analysis of Dante's terzinas (*Berliner Vorlesungen*, 1803–4) as constituting a triadic progression which would make this meter of particular value for prophetic poetry. Walzel praises Schlegel for his insight, but at the same time sees a fallacy in this particular analysis, because the terzina was successfully used for satiric, elegiac, and idyllic verse as well. "It would be foolish," Walzel writes, "merely for this reason to

---

28 "Das *Eidos*, etwas Geistiges, bedingt als ein Geistiges die äussere Gestalt des Schönen, in der Natur wie in der Kunst." (*Gehalt und Gestalt*, p. 154).
29 *Ibid.*, p. 178.

underestimate the significance of this experiment which attempts to deduce the claims of content from the conditions set by the structure." [30]

Walzel is indeed much concerned with numerical relationships in poetry and defends himself against the possible charge of indulging in a "romantic mysticism of form" by pointing to "unromantic" antiquity and its concern with numbers in the arts. He felt that because of the overwhelming concern for content in German literary scholarship, the necessary vocabulary for formal analysis had remained sorely inadequate. He lauds the use of classic rhetorical concepts in contemporary criticism of the Romance countries and feels that those concepts reach more effectively toward the ideal of "higher mathematics" than does the persistent concern of the Germans with philosophic content.

Walzel's poetics is meant to be applicable to both prose and poetry. However, the absence of meter and rhyme in prose prevents Walzel from making a specific distinction between "lower" and "higher" mathematics. Here he favors the application of the rhetoric of Roman antiquity. His attitude toward Aristotle appears to be negative throughout, a fact which can be discerned with great clarity when he deals with Plotinus. Stimulated by R. M. Meyer's *Stilistik* (München, 1906), Walzel dwells at length on the rhetorical concept of *numerus*. He views it as a pattern for prose, as real and precise as rhyme, rhythm, and numerical relationships in poetry. In discussing Charles Batteux's *Cours de belles-lettres* (Paris, 1753), he finds that the French critic's concept of *numerus* stems from Cicero's *De Oratore*. A consideration of several variant definitions of *numerus* finally leads Walzel to the conclusion that it refers primarily to the number of pauses in a given section of prose. Because it extends over a substantial part of a given work, the *numerus* must always apply to more than one sentence. At least those are the only two criteria which Walzel is finally willing to attribute to *numerus*, yet he claims with somewhat mystical certainty that they by no means exhaust its meaning, which can only be apprehended by means of "higher mathematics." We should remember at this point that "higher mathematics" is part of what Walzel means by *Gestalt*, and that the totality of *Gestalt* is embedded in *Erlebnis*, which ultimately is not susceptible to conceptual analysis.

Walzel acknowledges his debt to Eduard Norden's book *Die*

---

[30] *Ibid.*, p. 182.

antike Kunstprosa vom VI Jahr. v. Chr. bis in die Zeit der Renaissance (Leipzig, 1898). Norden had pointed to the great concern with form in classical antiquity and singled out this characteristic as the main distinguishing feature between Graeco-Roman and modern European literature. The Germanic peoples were particularly slow in accepting the rhetorical ornaments and formal elegance of the humanistic epoch. The Italians, on the other hand, accepted them readily and to this day show a great delight in polished, well-constructed phrases. Walzel deeply admired Norden's talent for distinguishing national traits in literary prose style and noted with satisfaction that he used classical rhetorical and stylistic concepts to achieve his end. Of crucial significance for Walzel's development was a lecture given by Norden (approximately 1911) in Berlin, which he attended.[31] In his search for some aid in his endeavors to find conceptual equivalents for *Erlebnis* and *Gestalt*, Walzel was struck by Norden's boldness in applying the terms "classicism" and "baroque" to Cicero and Tacitus respectively. He was elated to see that someone had the courage to release these concepts from their historical and chronological chains and apply them as formal categories to literary styles.[32] This was apparently the first time that Walzel had thought specifically about a method of elucidation which he later called *wecshselseitige Erhellung*. He did not embark on a full-scale development of the system until after he had come in contact with Wölfflin's well-known contrasting pairs of criteria in the fine arts. (See below, pp. 60–61.) It is not clear why Walzel should have foregone the use, or perhaps the expansion, of the ancient rhetorical vocabulary which he admired. Perhaps he felt that the insights achieved by modern literary scholarship (and by himself) called for a fresh approach in nomenclature as well.

His most persevering effort, prior to settling on an adaptation of Wölfflin's categories, undoubtedly centered on an extension of Dilthey's three intellectual types. He pursued with the utmost tenacity the goal which he had set for himself.[33] In a characteristic

---

[31] Published later in the volume *Die Bildungswerte der lateinischen Literatur und Sprache auf dem humanistischen Gymnasium* (Berlin, 1920), pp. 14 ff.

[32] "Ich lege vor allem Gewicht auf die Art und Weise, wie hier Cicero und Tacitus als ein Vertreter des Klassizismus und als ein Vertreter des Barocks einander entgegengestellt werden. Wie wertvoll mir solche Stilscheidung ist, soll noch später sich bewähren." (*Gehalt und Gestalt*, p. 197).

[33] To find ways for the application of Dilthey's *types* to literature, see also Rudolf Unger, *Aufsätze zur Prinzipienlehre der Literaturgeschichte* (Berlin, 1929), I, 49–87.

paragraph he wishes to make clear that *Weltanschauung* in literature is definable as *Gestalt*:

> I tried to prove by a few obvious examples that Dilthey's three types of *Weltanschauungen* may be made use of not only for the differentiation of poetic outlooks on life, but rather that the effects of type oppositions can be traced all the way to the technical peculiarities of the works. Certain shifts which presently or recently were observed in the artistic structure of the work, as well as in the outlook of the poet, can be handled readily by Dilthey's theory and thereby made more comprehensible.[34]

He had great difficulty, however, in effecting the transition from "type" to definable formal criteria, and moves on rather devious paths to achieve his end.

During his early years in Dresden (approximately 1912) he had attended certain technical demonstrations given by Eduard Sievers. Academic gossip had it that the eminent *Germanist* had become childish in his old age, for he insisted that literature be read "sometimes with arms stretched forward, sometimes with abdomen withdrawn," according to whether the author himself had or had not arched his abdomen in forming his sentences.[35] Walzel took Sievers' message seriously and admired his great sensitivity in classifying authors according to certain intuitively perceived "vocal" types. Indeed Walzel was aware of the extraordinary talent and sensitivity that helped Sievers in the preparation of critical editions; the specific tone of a poem was so vivid and distinct to Sievers that "he almost felt pain at the slightest deviation." [36] For example, Walzel believed that Sievers could easily determine which of the *Xenien* were Goethe's and which Schiller's. In fact Walzel himself had used Sievers' services when preparing an edition of Wackenroder's *Herzensergiessungen eines kunstliebenden Klosterbruders* to determine which passages, if any, might have been written by Tieck.

Walzel was aware of the limited use of Sievers' accomplishments for literary scholarship. No methodology could be derived from such divinations. What did interest him was the concept of "vocal type" based on the kinesthetic categories later developed by Ottmar Rutz in *Musik, Wort und Körper als Gemütsausdruck* (Leipzig,

---

[34] *Gehalt und Gestalt*, p. 96.
[35] *Wachstum und Wandel*, p. 157.
[36] *Ibid.*, p. 160.

1911). Rutz stipulated only three fundamental types to Sievers' six, basing them on certain combinations of vocal qualities, such as hard, soft, bright, dark, etc.

Herman Nohl, a disciple of both Dilthey and Rutz, tried to effect a merger of the intellectual categories of the former with the kinesthetic ones of the latter.[37] In Walzel's estimation, Nohl was unsuccessful, not apparently because of any theoretical difficulty of making the transfer from one to the other, but rather because he felt that Rutz's types represented *Weltanschauungen* which could not be equated with those of Dilthey.

How deeply Walzel was interested in such endeavors, however, is clearly indicated by the elaborate presentation of them in *Gehalt und Gestalt*. On occasion he identified completely with them and quotes with approval from Nohl's book. "He strives—as I do—for the 'definitive analysis of the elemental essence of the artistic entity.'"[38]

Rutz's first type is characterized by a "horizontal forward thrust of the abdomen, by a dark and soft voice, and by deep breathing." Its representatives include Napoleon, Goethe, Schubert, and Bruckner. The second type "thrusts the abdominal muscles above the hips horizontally backward, and arches its chest forward." The voice is high and soft. Frederick the Great, Schiller, and Beethoven belong to this group. Finally there is the type whose voice is bright and hard, and the abdominal muscles are pushed obliquely forward. Liszt and Richard Wagner, as well as the statues of ancient Greece, are proposed as examples.

To reconstruct body position and muscular tensions of individuals who lived in past centuries, is at best a hazardous undertaking, particularly if one considers the lack of photographic evidence. To make assumptions about specific vocal qualities, however, would obviously involve circular reasoning. Undoubtedly, such reasoning has taken place in the matter of reconstructing body postures as well; at least the generosity with which examples of one or the other kinesthetic type are given, leads one to expect it. In the case of the voice, however, there is no possible escape. An analysis of Goethe's voice, for example—beyond the casual, documented impressions of friends—could only be achieved by extrapolating from

---

[37] Herman Nohl, *Typische Kunststile in der Musik* (Jena, 1915).
[38] *Gehalt und Gestalt*, p. 96.

stylistic qualities of his prose or poetry. Thus Sievers claimed to "hear" differences in the quality of Goethe's voice according to the person to whom he addressed a poem or a letter.[39] Yet the only way in which such variations in tone could be determined would be by deducing them from Goethe's writings. The object of inquiry has been made into the premise of a new assumption.

It will be well at this point to recall Walzel's avowed opposition to psychological analysis of formal problems in literature; but he could hardly deny that muscular tone and bodily posture constitute physical responses to intellectual, emotional, or aesthetic values, that such responses are therefore neither logical nor metaphysical but clearly psychological and even physiological. Walzel appears to acknowledge this implication when he states that Rutz's theories show individual intellectual characteristics to be the ineluctable result of physical type. Yet at the same time he claims equal force for the opposite assumption, according to which the theory would also show the power of mind over matter. As evidence he adduces the notion that a work of art compels the beholder to assume a "typical" posture: "While Rutz in an unusual and novel manner subjects spiritual creativity to materiality, he also confirms the power of spirit over matter. . . . A painting, a plastic representation, a work of architecture—they all compel, as it were, muscular positions according to the laws imposed by their types and sub-types." [40] This observation closely resembles Dilthey's view, expressed in his poetics as early as 1887, that the aesthetic impression is analogous to the creative process, though only a "faded copy" of it.[41] This familiar "infection" theory does not constitute—as Walzel would have it—an example of the power of mind over matter. Rutz's theories, if applied consistently, would lead to a deterministic and psychological view of art and artistic creation to which Walzel had been so assiduously opposed.

The success or failure of Walzel's attempt to effect a transition from Dilthey's three intellectual types to their embodiment in formal elements in literature hinges on Rutz's kinesthetic types, or

---

[39] Eduard Sievers, H. *Litzmann und die Schallanalyse* (Leipzig, 1921), pp. 42 ff.

[40] *Gehalt und Gestalt*, p. 99.

[41] "Die eine selbige Menschnatur lässt nach denselben Gesetzen schaffende Kunst und nachfühlenden Geschmack entstehen, und beide einander entsprechen." (Wilhelm Dilthey, *Gesammelte Schriften, op. cit.,* VI, 191.)

rather on the acceptance of their relevance to *Gestalt*. Walzel himself abandoned his efforts in this direction by recognizing the failures of both Nohl and Sievers. "But the merger of Rutz's types with Dilthey's types undertaken by Nohl appears to me to have failed. It collapses even more decisively with the expansion of Rutz's teachings recently undertaken by Sievers." [42]

Since the only object of Walzel's inquiry into Rutz's types was to show convincingly the close connection between *Gehalt* and *Gestalt*, between *Weltanschauung* and aesthetic form, it seems odd indeed that so much space and praise were lavished on efforts which he himself recognized as failures. However, Walzel obviously felt that in due time such efforts would meet with success, because the failures of Nohl and Sievers were based on mere technicalities. Walzel never really questioned the validity of equating body posture with aesthetic form. That there might be crucial difference between kinesthetic responses and formal elements in literature is never brought up as a possibility.

Walzel's untiring search for a system of formal classification came to a conclusion with the experience of reading Heinrich Wölfflin's *Principles of Art History*.[43] Early in 1917, Walzel gave a talk to the Kant Society in Berlin in which he advocated the adoption of Wölfflin's formal categories by literary scholars.[44] On a number of occasions, Walzel expressed his gratitude to Wölfflin through whose book he had "learned to see," [45] a skill with which he had been preoccupied as early as 1890 when he was Leopold Andrian's tutor.[46] And in 1924 he still shows a similar concern. "One must learn how to see in order really to grasp the essential features of artistic structure." [47] The optical faculty appears indeed to play a preponderant role in Walzel's scholarly life. It is the "optic" view of Goethe which he prefers to the "haptic" view of the positivist school in the latter half of the nineteenth century (see above, pp. 21–22), and it is no accident that he received from the visual arts the concepts and terminology which he had been so earnestly seeking.

---

[42] *Gehalt und Gestalt*, p. 102.

[43] *Kunstgeschichtliche Grundbegriffe* (München, 1915).

[44] An expanded version of this talk was published as *Wechselseitige Erhellung der Künste* (Berlin, 1917)—hereafter cited as *Wechselseitige Erhellung*.

[45] See *Wachstum und Wandel*, p. 238.

[46] See *ibid.*, p. 48.

[47] *Wortkunstwerk*, pp. 101–2.

Looking back over his own intellectual development, Walzel writes in 1926:

> Soon after my first attempts to survey and utilize what had been accomplished so far . . . the great advantage effected through Wölfflin's *Principles* of 1915 became wholly clear to me, an advantage which scholarship in the fine arts, in its search for the essential artistic criteria inherent in a work of art, had gained over my own discipline.[48]

Again, the arts which properly depend on "seeing" are invoked as leaders in the quest for conceptual penetration of literature. Reciprocal elucidation or illumination among the arts is not a new idea. The term *wechselseitige Erhellung der Künste*, which Walzel first used in his lecture at the Kant Society in 1917, seems appropriate enough, when it is clearly understood that Wilhelm Scherer had meant something quite different when he spoke of *wechselseitige Beleuchtung* or *wechselseitige Erhellung*. Scherer's "illuminating" analogies, which are literary as well as sociological, move vertically through time, whereas Walzel's are taken from the same moment in history, and are on a horizontal line connecting all the arts.

Walzel finds much of what he wishes to develop in the romantic notion of synesthesia and refers only briefly to the ancient saying, "Painting is mute poetry and poetry is articulate painting," attributed to Simonides by Plutarch.[49] The *ut pictura poesis* of Horace is not used in Walzel's brief historical account, and a short discussion of Lessing's *Laokoon* culminates in the rhetorical question: "Yet does Lessing really condemn Simonides' idea lock, stock and barrel?" [50] Walzel's answer is negative, though the argument leading to it is less than convincing: the chief gain of *Laokoon*, Walzel holds, lay in the proof it gave of the strength of Simonides' argument upon which, after some two millennia, Lessing had found it necessary to launch his famous attack. Above all, however, the dictum generally attributed to August Wilhelm Schlegel that "architecture is frozen music," [51] its reiteration and particular phrasing

---

[48] *Ibid.*, p. ix.

[49] Plutarch, "On the Fame of the Athenians," *Moralia*, Loeb Library (Cambridge, 1936), p. 500.

[50] *Wechselseitige Erhellung*, p. 9.

[51] For an analysis of the controversy regarding the originator of this witticism, see René Wellek, "The Parallelism between Literature and the Arts," *English Institute Annual, 1941* (1942), p. 32.

by Schelling and Goethe, is used by Walzel to buttress his argument in favor of reciprocal illumination. Specifically Walzel is concerned with the usefulness and logical coherence of stylistic comparisons between the arts. He points to the fact that it is necessary, first of all, to isolate specific formal concepts observable in at least two arts. Of these, "rhythm" is an important example. To speak of rhythm in the visual arts clearly involves a transfer from music and poetry, but if agreement could be reached on a proper definition of this concept, then the controversy over the possibility or impossibility of transfer would soon be resolved. In the psychological camp of Wilhelm Wundt and his disciples working at the University of Leipzig, the possibility of such a transfer was categorically denied. Ernst Meumann, in an exhaustive investigation on the psychology and aesthetics of rhythm—with which Walzel was acquainted—held that the practice of transferring "rhythm" to the visual arts involved an unwarranted expansion of the concept.[52] On the other hand, Walzel could cite contemporary scholars who viewed mutual illumination along his own lines. Karl Steinweg, for example, was convinced that aesthetic criteria developed for the visual arts can and should be applied to poetry.[53]

There were also scholars in Leipzig who, in applying metrical and rhythmical designations to the visual arts, proceeded in the opposite direction. For example, August Schmarsow and his follower Wilhelm Pinder argued for the validity of rhythmical analysis in architecture, and thereby became opponents of the Wundt group. The University of Leipzig thus became the center of this particular controversy.

In an attempt to isolate and define rhythm in the arts, Schmarsow came to the conclusion that the dimension of depth is necessary to the perception of rhythm,[54] because only in three-dimensional space—so the argument goes—is it possible to obtain successive impressions which might properly be called rhythm. In a later publication, Schmarsow loses all restraint and freely applies terms of prosody to architecture. Thus he writes: "A rigorously closed strophic structure is the decisive criterion of Eastern church archi-

---

[52] See Ernst Meumann, "Untersuchungen zur Psychologie und Aesthetik des Rhythmus," *Philosophische Studien,* ed. Wilhelm Wundt, X (1894), 260.
[53] See Karl Steinweg, *Goethes Seelendramen und ihre französischen Vorlagen* (Halle a. S., 1912).
[54] See August Schmarsow, *Unser Verhälrtnis zu den bildenden Künsten* (Leipzig, 1903), p. 112.

tecture," [55] and subsequently, with a burst of extravagance, he proceeds to show how the eight-line Alcaic stanza, when arranged vertically, with its fifth line placed at the center and the last line arranged as a horizontal base, will yield the skeleton of a Greek palmetto ornament.[56] It must be said in fairness that Walzel does not go along with such arbitrary schemes. They appear to him as mere comparisons of moods, devoid of any critical usefulness.

It is clear that on the road to a full-fledged theory and application of reciprocal illumination, Walzel learned more from the Austrian philosopher Johann Friedrich Herbart than from his contemporaries, until he came under the crucial influence of Heinrich Wölfflin. It was Herbart who enabled him to obtain a clearly defined idea of rhythm quite independent of three-dimensionality. From Herbart's *Lehrbuch der Einleitung in die Philosophie* (1813) he learned that music and poetry may be "spread out before us like a painting," and conversely a painting may be experienced as though it were the product of a "transitory art," since we enjoy it by means of a succession of impressions.[57]

Considering Walzel's life-long concern with the activity of "seeing," one can understand that he was sympathetic to an aesthetics that would justify the systematic application of his natural bent. It appears to him to be the most significant, if not the only, avenue toward the proper appreciation of *Gestalt* in literature. The discovery, when it was new, was like a revelation to him:

> As for myself, I can only say that I feel as though scales fell from my eyes ever since I adopted the principle of seeing works of literature pictorially, and to seek from the images which offered themselves to me structural secrets which a work, after being merely read or heard, yields only with great difficulty.[58]

It is undoubtedly true that some aspects of Walzel's full-fledged theory of mutual illumination have much in common with certain concepts expressed by Worringer, though Walzel thinks of his former student chiefly as a precursor to Wölfflin. He knew that Worringer made the error of using the designation "gothic" as a synonym for "Germanic" or "nordic," a usage which had a prec-

---

[55] August Schmarsow, *Kompositionsgesetze in der Kunst des Mittelalters* (Leipzig, 1915), p. 97.
[56] Schematic drawing reproduced in *Wechselseitige Erhellung*, p. 24.
[57] *Ibid.*, p. 15.
[58] *Gehalt und Gestalt*, p. 280.

edent in Goethe's Storm and Stress essay, *Von deutscher Baukunst* (1773). What interested Walzel was not so much the correctness of the designation as the fact that it was conceived as one of two contrasting formal possibilities. Directly opposed to "gothic" was "classic."

Worringer developed both concepts with the help of ornamental designs, in order to eliminate, as far as possible, the element of "content." Both types of ornament show repetitive patterns: the classic ornament has calm and clear delineation with the groupings distinctly set off from one another. Repetitions frequently occur in reverse or in mirror-image sequences. The gothic ornament, on the other hand, which was at the center of Worringer's interest, showed an "infinite melody of line." [59] Repetition, in this case, was a form of intensification indicating a constant searching for an indefinite goal of intensity. Instead of being fairly self-sufficient units, the patterns would achieve their full significance only when merged into the whole. Worringer spoke of "addition" in classical ornament as against "multiplication" in gothic art of the same type. The terms "empathy" and "abstraction" were also introduced to designate, in a general way, any form of realism in the first case, and a removal from life and nature in the latter. For Worringer, Egyptian art belonged to the "abstract" category, and the gothic or Germanic type was supposedly an expression of the same artistic impulse. Greek and Roman classicism, as well as modern realism, belonged to the opposite pole of "empathic" art.[60] Walzel noted with pleasure that Worringer used freely the language of music and poetry to describe graphic ornaments. Correctness in each individual case was of less importance to him than confirmation of his own principle of polarity. The idea of opposite artistic impulses became the cornerstone of his theory of value, to be discussed later.

There was indeed a similarity between Worringer's opposites and Wölfflin's five pairs of formal contraries, though for the latter they were no longer "classic" and "gothic" but "renaissance" and "baroque." The focal points of differentiation, developed by Wölfflin, were so chosen that by their proper application, two basic stylistic modes could be most fruitfully and significantly distinguished. Following is a list of Wölfflin's five basic concepts:

　1. The "graphic" and the "painterly" (*das Lineare und das Male-*

---

[59] Quoted from *Wechselseitige Erhellung*, p. 27.
[60] Wilhelm Worringer, *op. cit.*, pp. 63 ff.

rische) refers to an emphasis on the line on the one hand, and to a greater exploitation of light and color on the other. In the "graphic" the accent is placed on limits and outlines; in the "painterly" there is a thrust toward infinity. The transition from renaissance to baroque painting involves a movement from the "haptic" principle to a greater exploitation of optical possibilities.

2. Correspondingly, the movement from "surface" to "depth" (*das Flächenhafte und das Tiefenhafte*) shows a tendency away from horizontal stratification toward an emphasis of the quality of depth, from the foreground to an increased concentration on the background, and finally from horizontal and vertical lines toward diagonals.

3. "Closed form" and "open form" (*Geschlossene Form und offene Form*). The former shows distinct demarcations and well-defined forms; the latter tends to cancel such limitations and direct the eye beyond itself. This pair is sometimes designated as "tectonic" and "atectonic."

4. "Multiplicity" and "Unity" (*das Vielheitliche und das Einheitliche*). In the configuration of a classical painting the individual parts carry enough weight to show a measure of independence. The parts are, of course, conditioned by the whole; no lack of integration is implied. Yet each part can be apprehended as an entity. In a baroque painting, on the other hand, the parts are more completely subordinated to an all-pervasive leading idea.[61]

5. "Clarity" and "Lack of Clarity" (*Klarheit und Unklarheit*). This pair of opposites borders on the "graphic" *vs.* "painterly" category, though the emphasis here is no longer exclusively on the line. Wölfflin is concerned with the tangibility of form in general. In classic art the idea of beauty is irrevocably tied to a full revelation of form. In baroque art the clarity of represented objects is relative.[62] Light, color, and composition are no longer pressed into the service of clarity, but are released to live a life of their own.

Wölfflin did not extend his criteria either to other periods or to other than visual arts. An extension into literary criticism was left to his followers. Moreover, Wölfflin did not regard his sets of criteria as a system of logical categories. Rather they represented five equally valid modes of seeing (*Anschauungsformen*), predetermined by evolving historical forces. It must be understood that, according

---

[61] Heinrich Wölfflin, *Kunstgeschichtliche Grundbegriffe*, 7th ed. (München, 1929), pp. 16–17.
[62] *Ibid.*, p. 211.

to Wölfflin, the expressed form, while traditionally involved in the imitation of nature, also answers the dictates of decorative principles and rules. Changes and transitions occur as much in the interest of decorative patterns as in the interest of faithfulness to nature.[63]

Wölfflin's is a theory of irreversible development in the visual arts. It is not necessary, of course, that a painting meet all five criteria of either the baroque or renaissance style. However, several of the criteria should always be discernible if the work in question is to be assigned to either one of the two periods. Groups of criteria are often so closely related that in many cases one can be said to imply the other.

Wölfflin's valuable observations exerted great influence not only in art criticism and art history, but in literary scholarship as well.[64] To Theophil Spoerri[65] and Walzel goes the distinction of having been the first to apply systematically Wölfflin's pairs of opposites to literature. Above all, however, it was Walzel who was not content merely to engage in a transfer of vague impressionistic data; he engaged in a strenuous effort to find logical correspondences.

Walzel was clearly right in asserting that German criticism had been preponderantly idealistic and ideological. The content of literature had long been the focus of attention, and critical analysis based on form was far more advanced in the visual arts than in literature. One can sympathize with Walzel when, time and again, he points to the extraordinary difficulty of converting feelings and impressions created by the literary work of art into concepts: "Art and science are once and for all opposites. To convert art into concepts is a difficult undertaking, but an indispensable one if cognitive statements concerning art are to be made." [66] It is undoubtedly true that there was a deplorable shortage of terms denoting structural elements in literature. The vocabulary of rhetoric had gone out of use, and for Walzel's purposes it was too closely associated with merely mechanical aspects of form; it included neither "inner form" nor "higher mathematics." It would have seemed natural to

---

[63] "Darum haben unsere fünf Begriffspaare sowohl eine imitative wie eine dekorative Bedeutung. Jede Art der Naturwiedergabe bewegt sich schon innerhalb eines bestimmten dekorativen Schemas." (*Ibid.*, pp. 17–18).

[64] Cf. René Wellek, *English Institute Annual, 1941, op. cit.*, pp. 36 ff.

[65] Theophil Spoerri, *Renaissance und Barock bei Ariost und Tasso. Versuch einer Anwendung Wölfflinscher Kunstbetrachtung* (Zürich, 1922).

[66] *Wachstum und Wandel*, p. 21. Cf. also *Geistesleben*, p. 87; *Wechselseitige Erhellung*, pp. 10, 42; *Gehalt und Gestalt*, pp. 139, 144, *et passim.*

devise a new technical vocabulary based solely on literary structural concepts.

However, Walzel was either unable or unwilling to do so. He could not directly convert his impressions into concepts, and hence proceeded in the opposite direction: he took over the ready-made terminology of the visual arts and used it to crystallize impressionistic data gained from literature. He believed this to be an excellent method, although his arguments in support of it seem curious. The critical vocabulary of a particular art, which is taken from concepts which are part and parcel of that same art, runs a great risk, according to Walzel, of introducing an unwarranted notion of value. For in keeping with his idea of the equivalence of two opposite poles in style, Walzel thought it of paramount importance that the critical vocabulary be neutral. He felt that even Wölfflin, in restricting himself to the field of the visual arts, came dangerously close to expressing biased judgments. For example, by stating that a painting could be more or less "painterly," the inherent implication would be that the *more* painterly one is to be preferred.[67]

Surely Walzel was mistaken in his view that such a linguistically conditioned pre-judgment would be unavoidable. If a prejudice should indeed be promoted by the common root in *Gemälde* and *malerisch*, it could easily be eliminated by substituting a term for *malerisch* which would convey the same notion. Should such a term be unavailable, a suitable paraphrase could certainly be found. However, even such a substitution would seem superfluous, because Wölfflin showed no partiality in his use of the word *malerisch*. Not only did the word have a well-defined technical meaning in the fine arts, but in addition Wölfflin exercised great care in circumscribing that meaning, never charging it with any a priori value judgment.

The necessity for an interchange of critical terminologies among the arts has not been established by Walzel. It is not clear whether he felt that the structure of a literary work of art is not accessible to analysis in its own terms, or whether he believed that the concepts necessary for such an analysis already existed, that they had been described and delineated, and were waiting only for someone to bestow appropriate modern names on them. Rather than answering this question, he simply assumed that the terminology developed for a particular art form would have aesthetic validity for *all* the

---

[67] *Wechselseitige Erhellung*, p. 66.

arts. Karl Vossler, in deploring the lack of success of scholars like Walzel in advancing the cause of reciprocal illumination, was well aware of the enormous difficulties.

> Scholars who are at all concerned with reciprocal illumination among the arts should know that they are thereby entering into the field of philosophic aesthetics. The merely philological or empirical observation or comparison, without philosophic reflection, may produce sundry results, but it cannot achieve reciprocal illumination among the arts; for what is lacking is the reflector, i.e., the pure concept, in which the arts can be mirrored and perceived as a single entity.[68]

If literature is to be illuminated by means of the visual arts, then by the same theoretical justification, another art might serve the same purpose. Walzel paid tribute to this unavoidable conclusion by devoting one chapter in *Gehalt und Gestalt* to a discussion of possible methods for the exploitation of musical concepts for literature. There is an account of how frequently such musical forms as the sonata have been successfully employed in poetry, and indeed how the structure of certain poems has often been illuminated by being set to music. It is an uncritical and rather sketchy account. Nowhere in this chapter does Walzel countenance the possibility that to a musician a poem may be mere material, a starting point from which the musical imagination can issue into unpredictable formal constructs which are subject, above all, to musical rather than literary analysis. The scholar would do well to avoid being governed by the musical version of a poem if he wishes to subject such a poem to a structural analysis.

Walzel cites with approval Otto Ludwig's characterization of most of Shakespeare's dramas as sonata-like structures, and Felix Trojan's discovery of parallels in literature for such musical devices as the *basso obligato* and counterpoint, as well as for dissonances and their resolution. Walzel does not note, however, that probably the majority of all dramas could be viewed as "sonatas," so long as no more than a division into three entities (theme, countertheme, and broader restatement of theme) is required as a basis for the comparison.

As for Felix Trojan's more specific analogies, they appear indeed to be witty, perhaps even inspired metaphors. They fail, however,

---

[68] Karl Vossler, "Über gegenseitige Erhellung der Künste," *Festschrift Heinrich Wölfflin zum siebzigsten Geburtstag* (Dresden, 1935), p. 164.

to contribute to an understanding of that which is specifically literary.[69]

In Walzel's relatively short treatment of music as a possible source for illumination, the device of the *Leitmotiv* is discussed in considerable detail. He apparently regards it as an inherently musical device, although one might well look upon the *Leitmotiv* technique as merely a specific application of the principle of repetition, used throughout literary history as a basic element of structure.[70] To be sure, it was used before Wagner, who gave the technique its ultimate refinement, but it entered music only when reference to extra-musical material—characters, situations, or events—was made.[71]

August Wilhelm Schlegel's Berlin lectures led Walzel to emphasize the desirability, and indeed necessity, of using harmony as well as melody in making the transfer of concepts from music to literature. From the relatively cursory treatment of music it is quite apparent, however, that Walzel's affinity to the visual arts is far greater than to music. Nowhere is there an affirmative experience caused by anything in music comparable to what he felt when he read Wölfflin. "For me it was a revelation when in the midst of my investigations whose preliminary results I am now presenting, I opened H. Wölfflin's *Principles of Art History*." [72]

The first application in criticism of Walzel's new insight was a structural analysis of Shakespeare's plays using two closely related pairs of Wölfflin's opposites, "tectonic and atectonic" and "closed form and open form," and arriving at the conclusion that Shakespeare is in the main a baroque poet.[73] Without going into the merits

---

[69] Felix Trojan, *Das Theater an der Wien* (Wien, 1923), pp. 18 ff.

[70] Martin Schütze dealt with the formal problem of the *Leitmotiv* as follows: "The use of the Leitmotiv type of repetition in literary composition, even though it was brought to a very rich and characteristic development by a later composer of romantic opera, namely Wagner, is not evidence of the romantic nature of the device of composition, but simply of the obvious fact that the literary structure of romanticism rested on the principle of repetition common to all the arts, and that romanticism tended to stress particularly those uses of repetition which were most effective in emotional intensification." (*Academic Illusions* [Chicago, 1933], p. 219.)

[71] Under "Leading Motif" the *Oxford Companion to Music* states as follows: "It [Leitmotiv] is, indeed, such an obvious means of connection between related passages of the libretto that it was bound to be introduced as soon as opera and oratorio were born." (London, 1938.)

[72] *Workunstwerk*, p. 315.

[73] See "Über Shakespeares dramatische Baukunst," *Jahrbuch der deutschen Shakespeare-Gesellschaft*, LII (1916), 3–35; reprinted in *Das Wortkunstwerk, Mittel seiner Erforschung* (Leipzig, 1926), pp. 302–25.

of such a designation at this juncture, suffice it to note that the idea of a "baroque Shakespeare" quickly found a large number of adherents in Germany as well as abroad.[74] The following year, in a talk held before the Kant Society in Berlin, Walzel engaged in a review and analysis of the principles he employed in effecting a transfer of critical concepts from painting to poetry. It was clearly his intention to build a strong case for his position and to persuade a philosophically-minded audience of the validity of his method. The immediate task was to justify the application of Wölfflin's categories to literature. As may be expected, he found no difficulty with the concepts of "multiplicity and unity" and "clarity and lack of clarity." They are easily applicable to all the arts and present no epistemological difficulties. Trouble arises with the second category, "surface and depth," because the application of this concept to literature is not unequivocal. Alois Riehl, for example, dealing with the same concept seventeen years earlier, had envisioned a different possibility of transfer.[75] He based his views on a theoretical work written by the sculptor Adolf v. Hildebrand, entitled *Problem der Form in der bildenden Kunst* (1893) and applied certain categories of "pure visibility" to literature. Thus the relationship between main level (*Hauptfläche*) and background level (*Hintergrundfläche*) in painting was seen as analogous to the juxtaposition of the opening and closing situation in a drama. Walzel, however, did not accept this analogy. Rather he saw the literary equivalent of the category in the hierarchy of personages in a drama, regardless of whether they appear simultaneously or in succession. Thus the classic French drama, and also Goethe's *Iphigenie* and *Tasso*, show the "surface" quality attributed by Walzel to the Renaissance. The number of characters is limited. Each figure is delineated with approximately equal clarity, and the function of each is well defined. There are no "receding lines" and no "diagonals." If, on the other hand, there is a profusion of characters, or if in addition to one leading personage there are others of lesser or indistinct rank in the hierarchy, as for instance in Shakespeare's *King John* and *King Lear*, or in Goethe's *Goetz von Berlichingen*, then the resulting effect would correspond to that of "depth" in the visual arts.

Much effort was devoted to buttressing and elaborating the principles employed in characterizing Shakespeare as baroque. It is, how-

---

[74] See René Wellek, *English Institute Annual 1941*, p. 39.
[75] A. Riehl, "Bemerkungen zu dem Problem der Form in der Dichtkunst," *Vierteljahresschrift für wissenschaftliche Philosophie*, XXII (1898), 109.

ever, not the second but the third of Wölfflin's categories which was the most important to Walzel in his discussion of Shakespeare's style. His critical perception was attuned to discover "closed" or "open" form, tectonic or atectonic structures. Undoubtedly the "surface and depth" category merges imperceptibly with them, but in retrospect Walzel felt that Wölfflin's third set yielded the essential insight.[76] Two tragedies of Shakespeare, *Antony and Cleopatra* and *King Lear*, served to reinforce Walzel's belief in the efficacy of his new critical tool. He began his essay on Shakespeare by praising August Wilhelm Schlegel for having introduced sculpture and painting in order to elucidate the contrast between classical and romantic art, and for showing that Shakespearean drama belonged to the latter category while the drama of Greek antiquity was more akin to sculpture.[77] He intended, however, to go beyond this comparison. His own application of the single category of "closed or open" (tectonic or atectonic) form appeared to provide the proper and adequate tool for the analysis of the difficult formal problems in *King Lear* and *Antony and Cleopatra*. These dramas, Walzel asserted, are in their essence closely related to the paintings of Rubens and Rembrandt. Thus with the utilization of a single morphological criterion, Walzel redefined traditional period terms. Corneille and Racine are classic dramatists because the form of their drama is "closed." Shakespeare is baroque because many of his dramas show "open" form. The "central axis" in the French dramas is the prerequisite for "tectonic" form. Shakespeare's plays on the other hand are based on "the diagonal" and are therefore "atectonic."

In his lecture before the Kant Society (1917) Walzel appeared still to be hesitant in places and even doubtful about the ultimate usefulness of reciprocal illumination. It was at this time that he had the important, but later forgotten, insight that two contrasting modes—while applicable to literature—by no means exhaust the possibilities, for clearly a painting may be "graphic" or "painterly," but it may also be neither.[78] This problem, and indeed the entire notion of reciprocal illumination, is treated with fewer scruples and even with extravagance in the later presentation contained in the more ambitious setting of *Gehalt und Gestalt*. In this work the author treats the principle as one established beyond any serious

---

[76] *Wechselseitige Erhellung*, p. 95.
[77] Cf. August Wilhelm Schlegel, *Sämtliche Werke*, ed. Eduard Böcking (Leipzig, 1846–47), VI, 157 f., 161 f., 185 f.
[78] *Wechselseitige Erhellung*, p. 60.

doubt, although he was still wavering with respect to the specific application of Wölfflin's categories. The opposition of "graphic" versus "painterly" continued to be troublesome. It could refer to the more or less concrete representation of the "visible," but it could also be used to distinguish two differing types of linguistic expression. Walzel felt that to limit the concept to either one of the two possibilities would seriously impair its usefulness.

There is little doubt that general comparisons are indeed possible among the arts. They may serve to evoke moods and provide interesting ways of looking upon a given work. Surely certain modes of painting, including Wölfflin's categories, may act as catalysts for the understanding of a poem—at least for those observers who have an intuitive affinity for both. Such metaphorical probings, however, cannot take the place of literary analysis; the fact that each literary work represents the solution of a particular structural problem must not be obscured. It is the business of the literary scholar to deal with both the problem and its solution. Any insistence on a one-to-one relationship between the formal aspects of one art and those of another tends to destroy what value there is in metaphorical elucidation, without thereby creating an acceptable new system of norms.

Under the impact of morphological analogies the usefulness of a period-term, such as "baroque," is seriously impaired, because the word is then no longer by necessity attached to a specific phase in the history of art. Indeed, as may be expected, Walzel saw the formal qualities not so much as symptoms of a specific moment in literature but, more important, as recurrent phenomena throughout literary history. He praised Eduard Norden for designating Cicero as classical and Tacitus as baroque (see above, p. 52), and saw no objection to the application of the same criteria to the antithesis of classic and romantic literature, as had indeed been done by Fritz Strich in *Deutsche Klassik und Romantik* (München, 1922).

It is certainly justifiable to see polar opposites of artistic expression, wherever there is a historical sequence of action and reaction, but surely the task of circumscribing or defining a literary movement would begin rather than end with the finding of opposed morphological criteria. Walzel showed great acumen when he noted that a poet may turn out to be neither "graphic" nor "painterly," but unfortunately he did not extend this insight to the other sets of polar opposites. Literary criticism is not greatly enriched by even the most elaborate system which in the end does little except to demonstrate that there is an eternal recurrence of action and reaction in art, and more particularly in literature. As René Wellek pointed out, a number of aestheticians who lived before Walzel had arrived at similar views without having to borrow concepts from the other arts.[79]

Walzel's tendency to describe the literary style of one period primarily in terms of a reaction to a preceding period is very similar to that of his former student Worringer, whose contrasting pair of "gothic" and "classic" or "empathy" and "abstraction" provided him with an approach to literary criticism and historiography. Empathy and abstraction are conceived as two equivalent poles of artistic sensibility. For Walzel, all literary history is a constant struggle between these two needs.[80] Similarly Worringer's "gothic," or "abstraction," or "geometric regularity," was diametrically opposed to and followed by "empathy" or one of several forms of realism.

Moreover, both Worringer and Walzel almost imperceptibly came to associate opposing pairs with criteria of value. Walzel's sympathies, like Worringer's, lay with "abstraction" in art. He felt himself still to be in opposition to the materialistic theories of the Scherer school as well as to the naturalism and impressionism carried over from the nineteenth century. From Worringer Walzel had learned to look upon all forms of realism as the art of "hitting the mark" (*das Treffen*). The expression appears frequently in Walzel's critical and historical writings and is used, almost always, in a derogatory sense. Thus in a chapter on impressionism he observed: "The art of hitting the mark corresponds, in the nineteenth century, to the rule of materialism and positivism, while the art emanating from a spiritual activity which is independent of outward reality, corresponds to a reawakening of the idealistic spirit." [81]

While in Dresden, Walzel welcomed the rise of expressionism, and he noted that Worringer's work had lent much support to the new movement.[82] He showed his partisanship by attributing "creative

---

79 "[Wölffin's categories transferred to literature] help us merely to arrange works of art into two categories which, when examined in detail, amount only to the old distinction between classic and romantic, severe and loose structure, plastic and picturesque art: a dualism which was known to the Schlegels and to Schiller and Coleridge and was arrived at by them through ideological and literary arguments." (René Wellek, *English Institute Annual, 1941*, pp. 58–59.)

80 "In Wirklichkeit stellt die Kunstgeschichte eine unaufhörliche Auseinandersetzung der beiden gegensätzlichen Richtungen dar." (*Wortkunstwerk*, p. 72.)

81 *Die deutsche Dichtung seit Goethes Tod* (Berlin, 1919), p. 156—hereafter cited as *Deutsche Dichtung*.

82 *Wachstum und Wandel*, p. 227.

spirit" to the new expressionist movement (*Ausdruckskunst*), and deploring, at least by implication, the absence of such spirit in naturalism and impressionism. He hailed the advent of expressionism as a liberation from the petty concerns of personal and social relationships. Above all he showed impatience with the impressionists' minute observation of psychic states, so prevalent among the authors of the *décadence*. He felt that by such probings they sought vainly to "explain God and the world," without realizing that these are inexplicable.[83]

To Walzel expressionism was a new affirmation of a theodicy, of that which is beyond the grasp of reason and emotion, and accessible only to an ecstatic state of mind. He wrote: "[The expressionist] reaches for God in intensifying transports of enthusiasm; and God is attainable only through stupendous spiritual ecstacy." [84]

With such unsecular words Walzel greeted the advent of expressionism. This movement, he felt, was genuinely Germanic (in Worringer's sense), and in its emphasis on the gulf between life and art, "baroque." [85] He did not hesitate, in the name of expressionism, to detract from the merits of romanticism and even of Goethe.[86] This early aversion to realistic and secular aspects of Goethe is undoubtedly related to Walzel's unwavering Catholicism. However at the same time, Walzel never lost his faith in Goethe as the very center and apogee of German literature. Hence a conflict arose in Walzel which he tried, for a long time unsuccessfully, to overcome. One of the attempts at reconciliation is contained in the pamphlet *Goethes Allseitigkeit* (1932). And in the last section of his memoirs, dealing specifically with his Catholic faith, he serenely concludes that Goethe and Catholicism are by no means antithetical, that on the contrary Goethe had reinforced and enriched his own faith in Catholic dogma.[87]

---

[83] *Deutsche Dichtung*, p. 191.

[84] *Ibid.*

[85] Walzel remarked about Fritz von Unruh's drama *Louis Ferdinand Prinz von Preussen* (1914): "Für die mächtigen seelischen Spannungen des neusten Barockgefühls blieb in Louis Ferdinands Brust Raum genug." (*Ibid.*, p. 329.)

[86] *Ibid.*, p. 192.

[87] "Mir musste es ungewöhnlich viel bedeuten, Goethe mit dem Katholizismus einig zu wissen, viel einiger, als er es selber jemals ahnte. Er hatte mir für den Bau meiner Weltschau so viel geschenkt, dass ich nun ganz hätte umlernen müssen, wenn Verwandtschaft von Goethes Weltbild mit dem des Katholizismus sich meinem Forschen nicht ergab. Nun durfte ich nach bestem Wissen und Gewissen sagen, dass ich Goethe nicht dem Katholizismus opfern, nicht eine mir ganz neue Weltschau an die Stelle der von mir allmählich errungenen setzen musste." (*Wachstum und Wandel*, p. 322.)

It is easy to see that Walzel does not always hold to scholarly impartiality vis-à-vis the two poles of artistic expression. And yet one of the central propositions connected with his system is the equivalence of the two poles. It is the artist and not the scholar, according to Walzel, who can legitimately be one-sided. The artist or poet or musician is necessarily the representative of one style, and his art would suffer in vigor and conviction if he adopted a style merely provisionally, as one possibility among several alternatives. The scholar, on the other hand, must use the polar system to create order out of a seemingly chaotic mass of literary products. The polar system will prevent one-sidedness in critical perspective because for each enunciated or implied aesthetic norm, an opposite one of equal validity must be assumed to exist either potentially or actually.[88]

Walzel had always admired Schiller's antithetical view of the world, and he felt that Hegel's tripartite, dialectic evolution constituted a similar type of thinking.[89] The assumption of a threefold instead of a twofold division was "merely a formal," not an essential difference in view.[90]

Once the principle of inclusiveness was established, Walzel could turn his attention to the business of value judgment. He wanted at all cost to eschew mere impressionistic procedures in this field and was convinced that the question of evaluation could not be solved "by banging one's fist on the table in outrage." [91] One would think that Walzel's extensive preoccupation with *Gestalt* in literature, and his exploration of formal analogies among the arts would finally have served him to accomplish a task somewhat more inclusive than the mere giving of a new formal justification for such period-terms as baroque, renaissance, romantic, and gothic. And one would expect

---

[88] "Es gilt nur, das Gegenteil des aufgestellten Ideals zu suchen. Dieses Gegenteil wird meistens an der Stelle zu finden sein, gegen die sich der Künstler ausdrücklich ausspricht. Tatsächlich ist das, was der Künstler verwirft, nur ein anderes Ideal von gleichem Lebensrecht. Wo der Künstler im Sinn seines eigenen und eigentümlichen Schaffens und zu dessen Schutz für eine einzige Möglichkeit kämpft und diese Möglichkeit begrifflich festlegt, da kann der Betrachter und Bewerter eingreifen, um die beiden entgegengesetzten Möglichkeiten zu bestimmen." (*Gehalt und Gestalt*, p. 115).

[89] *Ibid.,* p. 311.

[90] "Drei Typen statt eines Paares gegensätzlicher Typen aufzustellen, bedeutet nur in der Form, nicht im Wesen etwas Besonderes. Drei Typen lassen sich mühelos ins Paarige überführen." (*Ibid.,* p. 116.)

[91] "Ein Denker von dem Feinsinn und der strengen geistigen Schulung F. Th. Vischers konnte tatsächlich meinen, dass die Frage des Werturteils zu lösen ist, wenn man empört auf den Tisch schlägt." (*Ibid.,* p. 119.)

71

Walzel's greatest effort to be devoted to an application of his formal analysis to the all-important task of evaluative criticism.

Instead we find that Walzel utterly disregarded his own work in this field and contented himself with asserting the existence of a "time spirit" (*Zeitgeist*) as the only valid standard for the evaluation of literature. Such is the necessary conclusion to be drawn from the chapter on value judgment in *Gehalt und Gestalt*. Accordingly, the value of a work of literature lies in its efficacy in expressing such a time spirit, which is also the spirit of a national culture. The gauging of the cultural value inherent in the work would then be the irreducible task of evaluative criticism.[92] While such a method, based on "culture contents" (*Kulturinhalte*), appears to be relativism par excellence, Walzel strenuously insists that value judgment should transcend relativistic reasoning.[93]

The extreme difficulty of adequately defining a time spirit is well known. Walzel's polarity concept is of little help here, because variants within a period-style are not necessarily "opposite." The temper and manner of a period make complex and unwieldy patterns which may yield a fairly distinct impressionistic image, but can hardly be a reliable standard for critical evaluation. Indeed, the idea that an essential unity pervades all intellectual activities of a particular period is open to serious question. René Wellek notes how deceptive a facile theory based on the parallelism between philosophy and art often is.[94] That there is more than a hint of circular reasoning inherent in the notion that the value of a work of art may be gauged by measuring it against the spirit of the times in which it was written, has been shown by George Boas, who writes: "Artists make their time as other people do, and the notion that there is a time external to the events which takes place in it requires but a little reflection to be discredited." [95] It is as though in order to ascertain the correct length of a measuring stick, that same measuring stick were used as a standard for its correctness.

---

[92] *Ibid.*, p. 136. (Walzel's book, with the promising title *Grenzen von Poesie und Unpoesie* [München, 1937] is not a work on evaluative criticism but a history of romantic aesthetics.)

[93] "Ich hingegen möchte auf dem Wege zu festerer Wertung über solche Zugeständnisse an den Relativismus einigermassen hinausgelangen." (*Gehalt und Gestalt*, p. 143.)

[94] René Wellek and Austin Warren, *Theory of Literature*, 2nd rev. ed. (New York, 1955), p. 110.

[95] George Boas, *Wingless Pegasus* (Baltimore, 1950), p. 211.

The *Zeitgeist* plays a preponderant role in Walzel's historiograph-ical method.[96] The literary history covering the period between Goethe's death and the first World War is seen as a phase in the circular movement of a time spirit whose path always leads through the opposite poles of impressionism and expressionism, materialism and idealism, the art of "hitting the mark" and the art which transcends reality. Walzel asserted that the swing toward realism had its beginning with Goethe,[97] and moved inexorably toward its culmination in naturalism. "*Jung Deutschland*" and the realism of the 1850's are seen as way stations on this road:

> This . . . account of German literature of the nineteenth cen-tury will show how on the path leading from Goethe through romanticism and *Jung Deutschland* to the realism of the time around 1850, external reality was approached and powers of observation were sharpened, how in spite of occasional devia-tions and regressions this objective came closer and closer.[98]

Shortly after the turn of the century, however, there was a momentous change: "Once more the wheel begins to move . . . bringing about one of those great revolutions which guide man from one mode of viewing the world to the opposite mode." [99] At the time of Walzel's writing, naturalism had already ceased to be a dominant force in Germany, and expressionism held sway. Walzel looked for a new direction in intellectual endeavors, but especially in the arts, whose fundamental task it was to express the world view of their period.

Analogous to the change which was taking place in his own day—a growing rejection of scientific empiricism—Walzel saw the *Sturm und Drang* movement, Kant's critique of human reason, and Hegel's idealism, as a reaction against eighteenth century rationalism. The common elements in rationalism and materialism, such as a thorough skepticism toward metaphysics and religion, were so apparent to Walzel that, in his view, similar reactions to them were bound to occur in any period of the intellectual life of the nation.

It is apparent that Walzel's theory of literary values is based on a notion which leads him in a direction opposite to the one in which

---

[96] E.g., *Deutsche Dichtung.*
[97] "Goethe ist ohne Zweifel der Ahnherr des Realismus." (*Ibid.*, p. 161.)
[98] *Ibid.*, p. 155.
[99] *Ibid.*, p. 157.

he had moved with fair consistency all his life. The impetus which he had provided toward formal analysis was an important step toward establishing the autonomy of literature as an art. An alternative to viewing literature as a document in intellectual history had been provided. It is therefore doubly regrettable that in the crucial business of critical judgment, Walzel reverted to extra-literary criteria and thus to a method which in other phases of literary analysis he had helped to discredit.

BIBLIOGRAPHY

I. Works by Oskar Walzel

"Analytische und synthetische Literaturforschung," *Germanisch-Romanische Monatsschrift* (1910), 257–74; 321–41.

Deutsche Romantik, 2nd ed., 2 vols. (Leipzig, 1912).

"Deutsche Romantik in neuem Licht," *Zeitschrift für Bücherfreunde* (1922), 466–68.

Die deutsche Dichtung seit Goethes Tod (Berlin, 1919).

Deutsche Dichtung von Gottsched bis zur Gegenwart (Wildpark-Potsdam, 1927).

Gehalt und Gestalt im Kunstwerk des Dichters (Berlin-Neubabelsberg, 1929).

Goethes Allseitigkeit (Freiburg, 1932).

Grenzen von Poesie und Unpoesie (Frankfurt, 1937).

Leben, Erleben und Dichten (Leipzig, 1912).

Romantisches (Bonn, 1934).

"Über Shakespeares dramatische Baukunst," *Jahrbuch der deutschen Shakespeare-Gesellschaft*, LII (1916), 3–35.

Vom Geistesleben alter und neuer Zeit (Leipzig, 1922).

Wachstum und Wandel (Berlin, 1956).

Richard Wagner in seiner Zeit und nach seiner Zeit (München, 1913).

"Wechselseitige Erhellung der Künste," *Philosophische Vorträge veröffentlicht von der Kantgesellschaft*, XV (Berlin, 1917).

"Wilhelm Scherer und seine Nachwelt," *Zeitschrift für deutsche Philologie*, LV (1930), 391–400.

Das Wortkunstwerk (Leipzig, 1926).

II. Sources and Secondary Readings

Batteux, Charles, *Cours de belles-lettres* (Paris, 1753).

Benda, Oskar, *Der gegenwärtige Stand der deutschen Literaturwissenschaft* (Wien, 1928).

Boas, George, *Wingless Pegasus* (Baltimore, 1950).

Dilthey, Wilhelm, *Gesammelte Schriften* (Berlin, 1922–36).

Ehrenfels, Christian von, "Über 'Gestaltqualitäten,'" *Vierteljahrschrift für wissenschaftliche Philosophie*, XIV (1890), 249–92.

Enders, Carl, "Oskar Walzels Persönlichkeit und Werk," *Zeitschrift für deutsche Philologie*, LXXV (1956), 186–89.

Friedmann, Hermann, *Die Welt der Formen* (Berlin, 1923).

Goethe, Johann Wolfgang von, *Sämtliche Werke. Jubiläumsausgabe in 40 Bänden* (Stuttgart, 1902–7).

Hatzfeld, Helmut, "A Clarification of the Baroque Problem in the Romantic Literatures," *Comparative Literature*, I (1949), 113–39.

——, "Literary Criticism through Art and Art Criticism through Literature," *JAAC*, VI, 1 (1947), 1–21.

Herbart, Johann Fr., *Lehrbuch der Einleitung in die Philosophie*, 4th ed. (Leipzig, 1912).

Hildebrand, Adolf, *Das Problem der Form in der bildenden Kunst*, 3rd ed. (Strassburg, 1901).

Körner, Josef, rev. of Walzel's writings, *Literaturschrift für germanische und romanische Philologie*, XXXIX (1918), 17–26.

Ludwig, Otto, *Gesammelte Schriften*, ed. A. Stern and E. Schmidt (Leipzig, 1891).

Maync, Harry W., *Rechtfertigung der Literaturwissenschaft* (München, 1910).

Merker, Paul, *Neue Aufgaben der Literaturgeschichte* (Berlin, 1921).

Meumann, Ernst, "Untersuchungen zur Psychologie und Aesthetik des Rhythmus," *Philosphische Studien*, X (1894), 249–332; 393–430.

Meyer, Richard M., "Philosophische Aphorismen," *Germanisch-Romanische Monatsschrift*, III (1911), 497–98.

——, *Stilistik* (München, 1906).

Müller-Vollmer, Kurt, *Towards a Phenomenological Theory of Literature: A study of Wilhelm Dilthey's Poetik* (The Hague, 1963).

Nohl, Herman, *Typische Kunststile in der Musik* (Jena, 1915).

Norden, Eduard, *Die antike Kunstprosa vom VI Jahrhundert v. Chr. bis in die Zeit der Renaissance* (Leipzig, 1898).

——, *Die Bildungswerte der lateinischen Literatur und Sprache auf dem humanistischen Gymnasium* (Berlin, 1920).

Plutarch, "On the Fame of the Athenians," *Moralia*, Loeb Classical Library (Cambridge, 1936).

Riehl, Alois, "Bemerkungen zu dem Problem der Form in der Kunst," *Vierteljahresschrift für wissenschaftliche Philosophie*, XXII (1898), 96–114.

Rutz, Ottmar, *Musik, Wort und Körper als Gemütsausdruck* (Leipzig, 1911).

Scherer, Wilhelm and Oskar Walzel, *Geschichte der deutschen Literatur* (Berlin, 1917).

Schlegel, August Wilhelm, *Sämtliche Werke*, ed. Eduard Bocking (Leipzig, 1846–47).

————, *Vorlesungen über schöne Litteratur und Kunst*, ed. J. Minor, *Deutsche Literaturdenkmale des 18. und 19. Jahrhunderts*, 17–19 (Stuttgart, 1884).

Schmarsow, August, *Kompositionsgesetze in der Kunst des Mittelalters* (Berlin, 1915).

————, *Unser Verhältnis zu den bildenden Künsten* (Leipzig, 1903).

————, *Zur Frage nach dem Malerischen. Sein Grundbegriff und seine Entwicklung* (Leipzig, 1896).

Schütze, Martin, *Academic Illusions* (Chicago, 1933).

Scholes, Percy (ed.), *Oxford Companion to Music* (London, 1938).

Sievers, Eduard, *Ziele und Wege der Schallanalyse* (Heidelburg, 1924).

Spoerri, Theophil, *Renaissance und Barock bei Ariost und Tasso. Versuch einer Anwendung Wölfflinscher Kunstbetrachtung* (Zürich, 1922).

Strich, Fritz, *Deutsche Klassik und Romantik* (München, 1922).

Sypher, Wylie, *Four Stages of Renaissance Style: Transformations in Art and Literature 1400–1700* (Garden City, N.Y., 1955).

Trojan, Felix, *Das Theater an der Wien* (Wien, 1923).

Unger, Rudolf, *Aufsätze zur Prinzipienlehre der Literaturgeschichte* (Berlin, 1929).

Vossler, Karl, "Über gegenseitige Erhellung der Künste," *Festschrift Heinrich Wölfflin zum 70, Geburstag* (Dresden, 1935) pp. 160–67.

————, *Gesammelte Aufsätze zur Sprachphilosophie* (München, 1923).

Wahle, Julius and Victor Klemperer (eds.), *Festschrift für Oskar Walzel* (Wildpark-Potsdam, 1924).

Wölfflin, Heinrich, *Kunstgeschichtliche Grundbegriffe* (Berlin, 1915).

Worringer, Wilhelm, *Abstraktion und Einfühlung* (München, 1908).

❧ Emil Staiger ❧

ALTHOUGH EMIL STAIGER is not primarily interested in reciprocal illumination among the arts, it quickly becomes apparent from his practical criticism as well as from his theoretical work that for him music and poetry have the most intimate ties, whose discovery and isolation lead him to fruitful results in the interpretation of literature. For Walzel a literary work became most readily definable whenever it took on the attributes of a painting in his mind's eye. Lines, colors and shades, foreground and background, and even rhythm were visual elements which to him could most readily reveal the structural aspects of literature. And he did not suddenly embark on this approach with the appearance of Wölfflin's *Principles;* it was rather a life-long preoccupation with "seeing" which caused him to seize eagerly the opportunity for systematization afforded by Wölfflin's book.

Staiger's orientation, on the other hand, is distinctly musical. To him, thinking in terms of music is more than a theoretical means to the end of critical analysis. Staiger is well versed in musical theory and deeply concerned with basic musical problems. His book, *Musik und Dichtung* (Zürich, 1947) contains a collection of public addresses on musical subjects ranging from J.S. Bach to Arthur Honegger. Unlike Walzel, however, Staiger does not attempt to develop a methodology of mutual elucidation; only once does he touch even briefly on this subject, in an essay on "German Romanticism in Poetry and Music." [1] It is an impressionistic approach to the method by which broad similarities of musical and literary style are sug-

---

[1] *Musik und Dichtung* (Zürich, 1947), pp. 61-85.

gested, without insisting on a particular system for effecting the transition from music to literature.

The musical element is a steady undercurrent in Staiger's writings on literature. He employs musical terms (song, rhythm, tonic and dominant, key, etc.) to characterize poetry, and deliberately chooses expressions etymologically or semantically embracing both music and literature. For example, he shows a predilection for the word *Stimmung*, because even though when used in the sense of "mood" it is no longer felt as a musical metaphor, it will easily yield its musical derivation upon scrutiny.[2] He shows similar partiality toward such terms as *klingen*,[3] *mitschwingen*,[4] *Schmelz*,[5] and, as may be expected, one never need look far for the word *Musik* itself.[6] His musical training makes Staiger an extraordinarily sensitive interpreter of acoustic nuances in poetry. His gift perhaps comes closest to Sievers' brilliant though unreliable capacity for apprehending the finest shadings of individual style (see above, pp. 53–56). With Staiger the "musical" interpretation of literary language, particularly when dealing with romantic poetry, frequently brings unexpected and important insights. Such analyses as the one concerning a stanza from Brentano's *Romanzen vom Rosenkranz* are fine examples of Staiger's critical perception of sound patterns:

> In des ernsten Tales Büschen
> Ist die Nachtigall entschlafen;
> Mondenschein muss auch verblühen,
> Wehet schon der frühe Atem.[7]

Thus the entire first ballad is attuned to "ü" and "a"; and in the same way each of the succeeding stanzas has its two assonances like tonic and dominant, a never-ending alternation. But Brentano achieves his greatest effect when he not only maintains those assonances but also rhymes within each stanza. . . . Sixty-three stanzas thus follow one another and when we

---

[2] "Es gibt ein Wort, das ebenso wie die Musik die Poesie trifft: Stimmung." (*Ibid.*, p. 76).

[3] "Die Verse klingen leer . . ." (*Grundbegriffe der Poetik*, 3rd ed. [Zürich, 1956], p. 47—hereafter cited as *Poetik*).

[4] "Ob aber ein Leser mitschwingt, . . . das kümmert den Lyriker selber nicht." (*Ibid.*)

[5] "So rühmen wir an der lyrischen Sprache den 'Schmelz.'" (*Ibid.*, p. 70).

[6] *Poetik*, pp. 18, 30, 52, 70, 77, 81, *passim*.

[7] Clemens Brentano, *Sämtliche Werke*, ed. C. Schüddekopf (München und Leipzig, 1909), IV, 10.

finish reading we can no longer escape the hypnotic power of "i" [ü] and "a." [8]

As we shall see later, the pursuit of music in poetry is not without certain dangers, particularly when an attempt is made to convert immediate musical perception into theoretical norms. Thus "style" is to be considered generally equivalent to "rhythm" (both concepts are given special definitions by Staiger), and since the latter is descriptive of certain musical phenomena, the former becomes an essentially musical term.

Staiger is greatly influenced by a theory of musical style evolved by a follower of Eduard Sievers, Gustav Becking, whose chief work *Der musikalische Rhythmus als Erkenntnisquelle* (Augsburg, 1928) is invoked in the introduction to musical as well as literary essays.[9] Like Becking, Staiger sees in musical rhythm the ultimate element of poetry, which is not susceptible to further analysis. In the essay on "German Romanticism in Poetry and Music" he writes:

> Style in and by itself, a rhythm, an attitude, an archetypal human gesture, cannot be conceptualized. However, the imagination can encompass it and can be guided if the interpreter will make it his duty to describe the manifold aspects of the work of art always with a view to the one, the unutterable.[10]

The ineffability of rhythm and style gains added significance if one considers that Staiger believes their isolation to be the "crux of literary theory." [11]

Much of the attractiveness of Staiger's interpretative essays undoubtedly stems—quite aside from their attention to acoustical detail—from a wholesome flexibility and freedom from subordination to dogma, a refreshing characteristic growing out of a constant closeness to the text under consideration. Indeed, the flexibility of Staiger's literary elucidations stands in some contrast to his rigorous and sharply outlined concepts which are to serve as a basis for a new literary theory. Staiger's concepts, as presented in his re-

---

[8] Emil Staiger, *Die Zeit als Einbildungskraft des Dichters* (Zürich, 1939), pp. 34-35—hereafter cited as *Zeit.*

[9] "Alle Begriffe wie 'barock,' 'klassisch,' 'romantisch' werden durchaus in Beckings Sinn gebraucht." (*Musik und Dichtung*, p. 9.) See also *Die Kunst der Interpretation* (Zürich, 1955), p. 13—hereafter cited as *Interpretation.*

[10] *Musik und Dichtung*, p. 64.

[11] *Interpretation*, p. 164.

markable *Grundbegriffe der Poetik* are absolutistic and idealistic in an almost Platonic sense in that a work of art can never fully realize them, although it may more or less clearly reflect their essence. Such concepts are by necessity non-historical and are viewed *sub specie aeternitatis,* a natural concomitant of Staiger's position which allows for only three basic modes of poetry—the lyric, the epic, and the dramatic—representing the three possible modes of human existence. Such a "fundamental poetics," in Staiger's words, aims at being a "contribution to philosophic anthropology." [12] He does not wish to build an applied poetics in the Aristotelian or classic sense and is not concerned with definitions of literary genres based on historical models. Nor does his theory have anything to say on the choice of a particular form or subject appropriate to certain genres. Instead Staiger seeks to penetrate the stratum of the written (or spoken) word in a quest for an essence which would tie literature to the "basic modes of human existence." [13] Accordingly, the triad lyric-epic-dramatic may be seen as analogous to "emotional, representative, logical faculties," [14] or in terms of activities, to "feeling, showing, and proving," [15] and ultimately to the three temporal-existential categories of past, present, and future.

Staiger's claim for the ultimacy of such a system is reinforced by the suggestion that the temporal triad is also the motive force behind the development of language, from syllabic "cries of feeling" to denotative words, and from these to syntactically structured sentences. Each stage is analogous to the lyric, epic, or dramatic mode respectively.[16]

The dominant influence on Staiger's theoretical considerations is Martin Heidegger, and Staiger acknowledges his debt on numerous occasions. Staiger's poetics represents above all an attempt to show the relevance of existentialism to literary theory. Heidegger

---

[12] *Poetik*, p. 12.

[13] "Fundamentale Möglichkeiten des menschlichen Daseins überhaupt" (*ibid.,* p. 209).

[14] *Ibid.,* p. 208.

[15] "Fühlen, Zeigen, Beweisen" (*ibid.,* p. 210).

[16] "Es ist keine blosse Analogie, wenn wir, um das Verhältnis von lyrisch-episch-dramatisch zu erklären, an das Verhältnis von Silbe, Wort und Satz erinnern. Die Silbe darf als das eigentlich lyrische Element der Sprache gelten. . . . Im epischen Stil dagegen behauptet das einzelne, einen Gegenstand bezeichnende Wort sein hohes Recht. . . . Die Funktionalität der Teile, das Wesen des dramatischen Stils, ist ausgeprägt im Ganzen des Satzes, wo das Subjekt in einem Verhältnis zum Prädikat, der Nebensatz in einem Bezug zum Hauptsatz steht und ein Vorblick aufs Ganze nötig ist, um die einzelnen Teile zu verstehen." (*Ibid.,* pp. 20–25.)

himself had "not even hinted" at a theory of literary kinds, yet in his famous analysis of three Hölderlin poems, Heidegger had used the three time-dimensions, or *Ekstasen*, as an implied principle of elucidation. It remained for Staiger to work out the rationale for an existential poetics. One statement of Heidegger's perhaps more than any other concerning the existential role of time, serves Staiger as a significant point of departure: "Just as futurity makes understanding possible, and pastness the mood, so decay, the third constituent structural element of anxiety, has its existential meaning in the present." [17] This corresponds to Staiger's identification of the dramatic with the future, the lyric with the past, and the epic with the present. In addition to the fact that Staiger quotes Heidegger at a crucial point of his argument,[18] there is ample evidence that the philosopher's influence, particularly in earlier studies, is quite pervasive. In *Die Zeit als Einbildungskraft des Dichters*, published in 1939, the very first chapter heading, "Die reissende Zeit," indicating the essence of the "lyrical" mode, is taken over from Heidegger.[19]

In an article dealing with the progress of Hölderlin criticism during the Second World War,[20] Staiger offers his hitherto most comprehensive estimate of Heidegger, and it is clear—even within the limited scope of the essay—that considerably more is at stake than the proper interpretation of certain Hölderlin poems. One need only consider that in Heidegger's view—and Staiger does not disagree with him on fundamental issues—Hölderlin represents the poetic principle par excellence, and the poet's works can somehow be made to yield the underlying essence of poetry itself. Staiger recognizes that the growth of Heidegger's ontology is intimately connected with the latter's deepening interpretation of Hölderlin,[21] and he finds the crux of existentialism—the equation of Being and pure Time—most palpably expressed in Heidegger's essays on Hölderlin, above all in the one dealing with the hymn *Wie wenn am*

---

[17] "Wie die Zukunft primär das Verstehen, die Gewesenheit die Stimmung ermöglicht, so hat das dritte Strukturmoment der Sorge, das Verfallen, seinen existentiellen Sinn in der Gegenwart." (Martin Heidegger, *Sein und Zeit*, 2nd ed. [Halle a. d. S., 1929], p. 346—hereafter cited as *Sein und Zeit*.)

[18] *Poetik*, p. 220.

[19] Heidegger, *Erläuterungen zu Hölderlins Dichtung* (Frankfurt, 1951), pp. 37–38—hereafter cited as *Erläuterungen*. The ultimate origin of "reissende Zeit" is clearly the last stanza of Hölderlin's "Archipelagus."

[20] "Hölderlin-Forschung während des Krieges," *Trivium*, IV (1946).

[21] "In ständiger Auseinandersetzung mit Hölderlin hat sich Heideggers Ontologie allmählich umgestaltet." (*Trivium*, IV [1946], 211.)

Feiertage (1941),[22] about which Staiger writes: "The interpretation of Hölderlin's hymn may therefore be seen, at least to a large extent, to represent the ultimate basis of Heidegger's own thinking." [23]

On relatively minor issues Staiger occasionally shows a critical attitude toward his master. When discussing Heidegger's Hölderlin essays, for example, he rightly takes him to task for isolating the poet from the intellectual climate of his day and for regarding him as a kind of absolute, unhistorical phenomenon: "Hölderlin's isolation, however, is not restricted solely to his relationship to contemporary philosophy. Almost jealously Heidegger is bent on disavowing any effects of historical events upon the poet." [24] And he notes specifically that Heidegger ignored the impact of Hölderlin's contemporaries, Hegel and Schelling.

Another instance of a difference of opinion between Staiger and Heidegger—this time a particularly fruitful one—concerns an interpretative detail in Mörike's poem *Auf eine Lampe*.[25] The poem consists of ten iambic trimeters:

> Noch unverrückt, o schöne Lampe, schmückest du,
> An leichten Ketten zierlich aufgehangen hier,
> Die Decke des nun fast vergessnen Lustgemachs.
> Auf deiner weissen Marmorschale, deren Rand
> Der Efeukranz von goldengrünem Erz umflicht,
> Schlingt fröhlich eine Kinderschar den Ringelreihn.
> Wie reizend alles! lachend, und ein sanfter Geist
> Des Ernstes doch ergossen um die ganze Form—
> Ein Kunstgebild der echten Art. Wer achtet sein?
> Was aber schön ist, selig scheint es in ihm selbst.

Fair agreement is reached on the interpretation of the first nine lines. However, the last problematic line elicits differing views with respect to the meaning of *scheint*. Staiger intuitively decides on *videtur*, the lamp "seems" blissful, an interpretation which would stress the separation of the *persona* from the art object which is being contemplated. Heidegger, on the other hand, takes a purely Hegelian view, interpreting *scheint* as *lucet*: Beauty shines through the art object; it is illuminated throughout.

An exchange of letters between Heidegger and Staiger provokes

---

22 *Erläuterungen*, pp. 47–74.
23 *Trivium*, IV (1946), 212.
24 *Ibid.*, p. 213.
25 *Trivium*, IX (1951), 1–16; reprinted in *Interpretation*, pp. 34–49.

an additional comment by Leo Spitzer, who subjects the poem to a rigorous philological analysis.[26] He provides the most richly documented and the most convincing interpretation of the poem, particularly of the last line. By pointing to the influence of Swabian colloquialism, he shows that the *scheint* in the last line should be read "is beautiful," in accordance with the Swabian *scheinen*, "to be beautiful." The same type of approach leads Spitzer to regard the *ihm* not as an ultimate linguistic refinement to indicate something less confident than *sich*, but rather as a Swabian mannerism, so that the last line could be rendered by the following paraphrase: "But whatever is beautiful is blissfully beautiful in itself." The three interpretations, taken as a whole, represent to my mind one of the finest examples of thorough textual analysis. Each of the three scholars is able to contribute to the full meaning of the poem by means of differing analytical tools. In my opinion, Staiger's worry that the poem, as an integral art object, may suffer by such closely reasoned analyses, is unfounded.[27]

Yet such disagreements concern minutiae and do not affect the pervasiveness and depth of Heidegger's influence, attested to not only by commonly held ideas but even by certain stylistic peculiarities. When reading Staiger's *Poetik*, for example, one's attention is drawn to a penchant for separating well-known German compounds. Even when not separating them, Staiger will sometimes call attention to the basic meaning of one or the other of the component parts. This unusual technique is used for such words as *Ein-gebung*,[28] or *Vor-behalt*,[29] and the same intent is apparent, even without orthographic separation, in such a word as *Vorwurf*, which acquires a specialized meaning by the etymology of the Greek equivalent, *problema*.[30]

Such a "fragmentation" technique serves Staiger well in restoring words, rendered dim and tired by common usage, to a new purity of meaning. As our examples show, the original unmerged state of

---

[26] Leo Spitzer, "Wiederum Mörikes Gedicht 'Auf eine Lampe,'" *Interpretation*, pp. 133–47.

[27] See Staiger's notes to Spitzer's article, *ibid.*, p. 147.

[28] "[der lyrische Dichter] überlässt sich—das will buchstäblich verstanden sein—der Ein–gebung." (*Poetik*, p. 24.)

[29] ". . . dass das Herz . . . ohne Vor-behalt, im eigentlichsten Wortverstande, sich dem Strom des Daseins überlässt. . . . " (*Meisterwerke deutscher Sprache*, 2nd ed. [Zürich, 1948], p. 19.)

[30] "Unter 'Problem' verstanden wir den 'Vorwurf' im wörtlichen Sinn des Begriffs, das Vorgeworfene, das der Werfende einzuholen berufen ist." (*Poetik*, pp. 174–75).

the compounds is meant to illuminate the structure of the concept to be discussed. Etymology is pressed into the service of conceptual analysis. A considerable dependence on this device is one of the more striking characteristics of Heidegger's and Staiger's style, though in the latter less violence is done to general usage. It is part of Staiger's fluid and immensely adaptable expository style. The following two passages from Heidegger may serve as a suitable means for comparison:

> Das Seiende, das den Titel Da-sein trägt, ist "gelichtet". Das Licht, das diese Gelichteheit des Daseins konstituiert, ist keine ontisch vorhandene Kraft. . . .

> Die thematische Analyse der zeitlichen Konstitution des In-der-Welt-seins führt zu den Fragen: in welcher Weise ist so etwas wie Welt überhaupt möglich, in welchem Sinne *ist*, Welt, was und wie transzendiert die Welt, wie "hängt" das "Unabhängige," innerweltliche Seiende mit der transzendierenden Welt "zusammen"? [31]

Heidegger shows a curious faith in the significance of German word origins. Leo Spitzer takes note of Heidegger's procedure and is justly skeptical of its validity. He refers to certain of the philosopher's phrases as "precious verbal pomp" (*preziöser Wortprunk*) [32] and writes:

> Many philosophical readers of Heidegger have been puzzled again and again by the use of etymology as a mode of thought (and especially by the use of *German* etymology for the exploration or documentation of universal circumstances). For the philologist it is a source of merriment to see how the customary verbal mesh of philosophy is spread out over philologically doubtful matters. . . . [33]

In our effort to obtain a clear understanding of Staiger's views, we are greatly helped by his introduction to the second and third editions of his *Poetik* where the need for a newly conceived, modern poetics is persuasively argued, and again by an epilogue which constitutes a kind of final apologia and a vigorous defense against

---

[31] *Sein und Zeit*, pp. 331, 350. The two passages were left untranslated because the linguistic points apply only to German.

[32] Leo Spitzer, *Interpretation*, p. 137.

[33] *Ibid.*, p. 143.

86

critical attacks.[34] As a result we are in a better position than the reviewers of the first edition of the *Poetik* (1946), because they were subject to certain misunderstandings—particularly with respect to the relationship of the adjectives *lyric, epic, dramatic* to their respective nouns—which have since been resolved by fuller explanations which Staiger added to the edition of 1951. Because Staiger shows a clear predilection for "the lyrical" we will first concentrate on this concept. Much of what is meant by "epic" and "dramatic" may then receive illumination by extension.

It has been stated that Staiger is not interested in collecting literary models or examples for the purpose of abstracting common characteristic qualities. He holds this method of determining literary kinds of genres to be confusing and not of great value:

> [Poetic theory] must . . . make comparisons between ballads, songs, hymns, odes, sonnets, epigrams, trace each of these genres through one or two millennia and then discover something which is common to all of them, and from that something arrive at the concept of lyric poetry. This concept, however, which holds true for all instances can never be anything but a matter of indifference.[35]

Similarly Heidegger writes:

> But is it ever possible to derive the general essence of poetry from the work of an individual poet? Actually, the general, i.e., that which is valid for many instances, can be gained only by means of a comparative consideration . . . but this general quality which is equally valid for all special cases, is always something indifferent and can never be of the essence. . . .[36]

To Heidegger as well as to Staiger, the essence of the poetic phenomenon can be revealed by the study of a single poet. Staiger observes that the "lyrical" mode can be felt, intuited, and experienced in the process of reading even small selections of German romantic poetry. Characteristically he writes: "And if I were asked according to what notion I would call a poem "lyrical," I would

---

[34] Compiled from lectures held in Oxford in 1948 and added to the second edition (1951) of *Poetik*.

[35] *Poetik*, pp. 7–8.

[36] From the chapter "Hölderlin und das Wesen der Dichtung," which is a reprint of a lecture given in 1936 in Rome. (*Erläuterungen*, pp. 31–39).

say, according to that which has been revealed to me by such poems." [37]

So long as the nature of the common elements in a particular group of poems is defined and characterized—as indeed Staiger has admirably done—a valuable contribution is made toward understanding and experiencing the spirit conveyed in such poems. Staiger has provided us with a new and precise focus on the lyrical poetry of German romanticism, above all by his keen perception of musical and rhythmical elements in poems by Goethe, Brentano, and Eichendorff. A difficulty arises, however, when Staiger elevates the insights gained from the poetry of a particular period to unalterable principles of ultimate validity. Surely German romanticism with all its antipathy to neo-classical forms was no less subject to literary conventions than other movements of comparable scope; to regard its "lyrical" standard as the supreme model for all would seem to be a somewhat hazardous procedure. Yet in the epilogue to the *Poetik* Staiger writes: "We derive the essence of the "lyrical" from romantic poetry, from poems by Goethe and from others which resemble them." [38] Staiger is working not merely towards a new definition of the conventional lyric, epic, and dramatic categories. The criteria by which they are traditionally recognized appear to him to be superficial and inconsequential. Too many variant styles and feeling-tones are lumped together in such categories. To say that lyrical poems are poems of small size, that dramas are pieces written for the stage, and epics long poems dealing with an action to be read or recited, would hardly constitute a contribution to a meaningful poetics. For the fact is that a short poem may be more "dramatic" than "lyrical," a work written for the stage more "lyrical" than "dramatic," etc. It is the quality rather than the kind which Staiger holds to be truly significant.

It is possible—and Staiger acknowledges this fact—that traditional poetics may take into account the apparent contradictions between quality and basic kind. A scholar like Julius Petersen, taking up a suggestion by Goethe (see p. 91), carefully distinguishes between basic literary kinds and genres. The former refer again to the well-known triad, whereas the smaller subdivisions, such as fable, ballad, idyll, satire, etc., are to be regarded as intermediary stages between the major categories. Petersen asks his readers to visualize the divisions of literature as a wheel with three

[37] *Poetik*, pp. 239–40.
[38] *Ibid.*, p. 243.

main spokes representing the basic kinds which divide the wheel into three groups of genres.[39] A movement around the axis may signify differences in gradations from subjectivity to objectivity: lyric to epic to dramatic—or from representations of material (*stoffartig*) elements to those of conditions (*Zustände*): epic to dramatic to lyric. Goethe's *Werther*, for example, is an epic work with lyrical tendencies in the first part and dramatic elements in the second; Dante's *Divine Comedy*, a "transfixed vision," is an epic with lyrical tendencies.[40]

Such a scheme, however, does not satisfy Staiger because Petersen advances no compelling reason for giving any predominance of the epic, lyric, and dramatic kinds over the various genres. Petersen's suggestion that the criterion of simplicity should apply to the basic kinds is unconvincing; for example, one can show that a prayer or an epigram may be fully as "simple" as an epic. Nor would there be —in the absence of an ontological foundation—any reason why future poets might not introduce new basic categories, which would vitiate the usefulness of Petersen's wheel. Staiger's insistence on a recognizable identification of "philosophical anthropology" with a poetics must not be forgotten.

One of the basic dilemmas of literary theory makes itself felt at this point. One may altogether deny the validity of a traditional poetics by regarding literary kinds or genres as illusory and ir- relevant to critical evaluation. In this case the aesthetic artifact may be studied by referring to the nature of "intuitive" and "expressive" knowledge. Curiously Staiger makes no specific men- tion of Croce's position or of any other nominalistic view, which looks upon each genuine work of art as being totally unrelated to old traditions or period-styles.[41]

At the other extreme, it is possible to ignore the connection between the poet and his work, to label the work according to its form, and to pass judgment largely according to the faithfulness with which the work conforms to its genre.

Staiger maintains that the bond between a work of literary art and human nature must not be severed. The inclusion of such a con-

---

[39] Julius Petersen, *Die Wissenschaft von der Dichtung* (Berlin, 1939), I, 124.
[40] *Ibid.*, p. 126.
[41] In the chapter "Historicism and Intellectualism," Croce writes: "The philosophical condemnation of artistic and literary kinds is found in the formulation and demonstration of what artistic activity has always done and good taste always recognized." (Benedetto Croce, *Aesthetic*, tr. Douglas Ainslee [New York, 1955], p. 37.)

tinuum in no way negates the possibility of a poetics. To break the tie with "philosophic anthropology," on the other hand, would inevitably lead to a rigid and stultifying scheme out of touch with the living body of literature. Julius Petersen, by failing to base his vision of literature on philosophic premises, is subject, according to Staiger, to intellectual sterility.

The first position, calling for an "unprejudiced" approach to each work of art, without reference to genre, is based on a semantic confusion arising from seeing in such adjectives as "lyric," "epic," and "dramatic," a much closer connection to their respective nouns than is in fact present. The adjectives are valid designations of an intrinsic aesthetic quality. If that were not so, it would be a blatant tautology to characterize a drama as "dramatic." It is only the noun which constitutes an external label. The adjectives may well serve as building stones for a new poetics.

The extreme formalist position, on the other hand, must be avoided because it leads to a "Babylonian confusion." A multiplicity of genres, the merging of one with the other, the possible creation of new genres, are apt to present a chaotic landscape with concepts strewn about "helter skelter as ruins of old poetic theories which have lost their foundation." [42]

The poetics of Staiger represent an attempt to resolve the impasse by pointing to three "modes of being" which underlie all imaginative literature. Both horns of the dilemma are thereby avoided: the connection between literature and human existence has been taken into account, and at the same time the number of basic kinds has been ontologically established; the danger of a chaotic and arbitrary increase of genres has been overcome.

The division of literature into three basic kinds is of course not new. Plato and Aristotle make their distinctions according to "manner of imitation": lyric poetry is an imitation of the poet's own *persona*; in the drama, the poet's *persona* is not in evidence at all. Epic poetry is a mixture of the two.[43] Irene Behrens showed that a specific doctrine of basic literary kinds did not arise until the end of the eighteenth century.[44] Only with the German romantics and ultimately with Hegel, did the three fundamental human attitudes,

---

[42] *Poetik*, p. 235.

[43] See Plato, *Republic* III; Aristotle, *Poetics* III. For a detailed discussion, see James J. Donohue, *The Theory of Literary Kinds* (Dubuque, Iowa, 1943).

[44] Irene Behrens, "Die Lehre von der Einteilung der Dichtkunst," *Beihefte zur Zeitschrift für Romanische Philologie*, XCII (1940), pp. 192, 202.

as expressed in the arts, become of overwhelming importance. Discussions of specific genres became submerged in speculations about the significance of the poetic, or simply artistic, utterance in the ultimate scheme of things.[45] It is likely that through the immense authority of Goethe the new approach to literary theory became of decisive and lasting importance. Although similar genre theories by F.W.J. Schelling and Jean Paul also exercised a vast influence,[46] there is no doubt that a number of twentieth-century German scholars working for the renewal of a poetics still look upon Goethe as their point of departure. In Goethe's *Noten und Abhandlungen zum West-östlichen Divan* (1819) there are two short chapters dealing with literary genre. In them Goethe expresses his belief that a principle should be found by which genre terms, such as ballad, fable, idyll, etc., might be arranged in an aesthetically significant manner, and comes to the conclusion that there are only three "natural" forms (*Naturformen*) of literature: the epic, the lyric, and the dramatic.[47] While recognizing that few of the *Naturformen* ever appear unmixed, he feels that they are quite recognizable and that therefore all genres and subdivisions can be placed in greater or lesser proximity to one of them, and suggests that they be grouped in a circle in which the *Naturformen* appear as radii and the segments be filled by the appropriate genres.[48] The elaboration of Goethe's suggestion by Julius Petersen has already been discussed. Emil Ermatinger is equally conversant

---

[45] See, e.g., Fr. Schlegel: "Die einzige [dorische] Form ist Lyrik (so wie Epos ausschliesslich Ionische Form, und Drama Athenische ist); und man darf nie vergessen, dass diese nichts anderes ist als der poetische Teil der Musik." *Friedrich Schlegel: seine prosaischen Jugendschriften*, ed. Jakob Minor, 2 vols. (Wien, 1882), II, 348.
See also *ibid.*: "Das lyrische Gedicht ist für Heroen. Das epische Gedicht ist für Menschen. Der Heros ist lyrisch, der Mensch episch, der Genius dramatisch. Der Mann lyrisch, die Frau episch, die Ehe dramatisch."
[46] Schelling compares the lyric to music, the epic to painting, and the drama to sculpture. See *Sämtliche Werke*, 14 vols. (Berlin, 1856–61), V, 640. Jean Paul, in his *Vorschule der Aesthetik*, associates the epic with the past, drama with future, and lyric with present. (See *Sämtliche Werke*, ed. Eduard Berend [Berlin, 1909], XI, 254).
[47] Johann Wolfgang von Goethe, *Sämtliche Werke, Jubiläumsausgabe in 40 Bänden* (Stuttgart, 1902–7), V, 223.
[48] "Man wird sich aber einigermassen dadurch helfen, dass man die drei Hauptelemente in einem Kreis gegen einander über stellt und sich Musterstücke sucht, wo jedes Element einzeln obwaltet. Alsdann sammle man Beispiele, die sich nach der einen oder nach der anderen Seite hinneigen, bis endlich die Vereinigung von allen dreien erscheint, und somit der ganze Kreis geschlossen ist." (*Ibid.*, V, 224.)

THREE MODES OF CRITICISM

with the triad epic-lyric-dramatic and believes that these basic forms have prototypes which may for all time serve to determine literary genres.[49] Karl Viëtor noted that Ermatinger, in considering the *Naturformen* absolute concepts preceding experience, misinterpreted Goethe. He shows that on the contrary, Goethe insisted that all concepts be arrived at inductively.[50] A psychological justification for the existence of the *Naturformen* is offered by Robert Hartl's book *Versuch einer psychologischen Grundlegung der Dichtungsgattungen* (Wien, 1924). Deliberately proceeding from Kant, he derives the basic modes from the three categories of the mind: drama is related to the will (*Begehrungsvermögen*), epic to thought (*Erkenntnisvermögen*), lyric to emotion (*Gefühl*).[51]

Once Staiger has presented his argument for the desirability of an "anthropological" poetics, he shows great concern with certain basic problems in methodology. For example, he finds it necessary to justify and defend a kind of circular reasoning which he had used to obtain his results. Concepts are developed by abstracting from pertinent detailed data, yet such data cannot be properly understood, or even selected, without a preceding general grasp of the whole. The special concepts of "lyric," "epic," and "dramatic" were undoubtedly developed in this fashion, moving back and forth between interpretative detail and basic concept. This method is not new and has for some time been generally accepted. Staiger is able to cite persuasive statements by such eminent scholars as Dilthey (in his essay on hermeneutics),[52] and above all by Heidegger, in

---

[49] Cf. Emil Ermatinger, *Philosophie der Literaturwissenschaft* (Berlin, 1930), p. 371.

[50] Karl Viëtor, "Die Geschichte der literarischen Gattungen," *Geist und Form* (Bern, 1952), p. 302.

[51] An interesting sidelight on the place of basic categories in all the arts is provided by Stephen Dedalus in Joyce's *Portrait of the Artist as a Young Man*, which appeared in 1916, before this notion became of renewed major concern among German scholars. Clearly Goethe thought the sequential order to be of no great consequence and proposed the arbitrary series: epic, lyric, drama. Joyce's Stephen Dedalus, however, expresses the idea of a Hegelian pre-ordained movement from lyric to dramatic: ". . . you will see that art necessarily divides itself into three forms progressing from one to the next. These forms are: the lyrical form, the form wherein the artist presents his image in immediate relation to himself; the epical form, the form wherein he presents his image in mediate relation to himself and to others; the dramatic form, the form wherein he presents his image in immediate relation to others." (Viking Compass Books [New York, 1958], pp. 213–14.)

[52] "Aus den einzelnen Worten und deren Verbindungen soll das Ganze eines Werkes verstanden werden, und doch setzt das volle Verständnis des einzelnen schon das Ganze voraus." (Wilhelm Dilthey, *Gesammelte Schriften* [Leipzig, 1922–36], V, 330).

support of such circular logic. Heidegger moreover takes the bolder step of regarding the circle by no means as a *vitiosum* but on the contrary, as a "positive possibility for obtaining fundamental insights." [53] A very similar type of circular reasoning has also come under the scrutiny of René Wellek and been deemed unavoidable in the definition of literary periods. Not to grasp the efficacy of this method is apt to lead to the unwarranted introduction of extra-literary values, such as the Hegelian triadic progression, or of other idealistic systems.[54]

We would do well not to take exception to the logical circle implicit in Staiger's *Grundbegriffe*. It represents a welcome acceptance of a personal perspective, while at the same time it is likely to produce a poetics based on the substance of literature itself. "Through the matter itself!" Staiger writes. "This is how we tackle an investigation . . . to maintain exactly the course along which the apprehension and understanding of a poem actually moves." [55]

However, it appears to me, that Staiger pushes the results of his reasoning beyond its intrinsic limitation, for surely an abstraction like "the lyrical" can be expected to apply to periods other than the romantic and to languages other than German. Moreover Staiger's "anthropological" absolutes make no allowances for the fact that even the basic literary kinds are subject to change with the advent of new literary forms. Nor is the problem solved by the introduction of a dichotomy between the "impure" literary work on the one hand and a substratum of ultimate and pure concepts on the other, as indicated in passages like the following: "But it is not a meaningless undertaking to throw open the question concerning the essence of the lyric, epic and dramatic modes. For these qualities are simple, and their stability is not disturbed by the flickering and wavering characteristics of individual works." [56] On the contrary, it seems to me that the dichotomy impairs the unity of the poetic artifact in a mannner reminiscent of Plato's double focus, one directed toward circles, triangles, and cubes, the other toward their imperfect projections in the sensible world. It would seem more fruitful to apply the historicism of Vico and to realize that an artifact, such as a lyrical poem, has reality and a set of qualities only in

---

[53] *Sein und Zeit*, p. 153.

[54] Cf. René Wellek and Austin Warren, *Theory of Literature*, 2nd ed. (New York, 1956), p. 247.

[55] *Zeit*, p. 19.

[56] *Poetik*, pp. 237–38.

terms of its particular period in literary history.[57] In an excellent article published in 1931, Karl Viëtor showed a keen awareness of the pitfalls surrounding a method which develops literary categories from too small a segment of literary history.[58] He specifically criticized the procedure recommended by Emil Ermatinger in his essay "Das Gesetz der Literaturwissenschaft": [59]

> . . . if the situation were as Ermatinger thinks, then one would have to base one's decision as to genre on the type.[60] The type could in this case not be based on experience, as in Goethe, but would have to precede experience. I would not know where to obtain it except by considering a single work as exemplary and to raise it to the purity of a normative type. A history of verse, however, which . . . uses Goethe's poetry as a norm, would result in a complete distortion of the historical picture. . . . Clearly no single work can in fact be the representative of a genre.[61]

The gulf between permanent aesthetic norms on the one hand and the flux of historical development on the other may be bridged by regarding literary categories as institutions of the kind Harry Levin proposes.[62] While membership in such an institution would naturally imply identification with it, it would by no means signify conformity. The most "basic" institutions have the greatest durability, although nothing guarantees their permanence. Classical and medieval epics, both of the oral and written tradition, Klopstock's *Messias* and Milton's *Paradise Lost*, may all claim membership in the institution of the epic, which would not exist without the body of works that make up the epic tradition. A critical evaluation of these works may properly make reference to the institution of the epic. Each new genuine work of art changes the total character of

---

[57] "The nature of things is nothing but their coming into being (*nascimento*) at certain times and in certain fashions. Whenever the time and fashion is thus and so, such and not otherwise are the things that come into being." (Giambattista Vico, *The New Science*, tr. T. G. Bergin and M. H. Fisch [Ithaca, 1948], p. 58.)

[58] Viëtor is in substantial agreement with Günther Müller's "Bemerkungen zur Gattungspoetik," *Philosophischer Anzeiger*, III (1929), 129–47.

[59] Emil Ermatinger, *op. cit.*, pp. 331–75.

[60] The word *Typus* denotes a concept closely related to Staiger's *Grundbegriff*.

[61] Karl Viëtor, *op. cit.*, p. 303.

[62] "Literature as an Institution," *Accent*, VI (1946), 150–69.

the institution, as T.S. Eliot fully recognized in his essay of 1919, "Tradition and the Individual Talent":

> The existing monuments form an ideal order among them-selves, which is modified by the introduction of the new (the really new) work of art among them. The existing order is complete before the new work arrives. . . .Whoever has approved this idea of order, of the form of European, of English literature, will not find it preposterous that the past should be altered by the present as much as the present is directed by the past.[63]

An echo of this influential statement is audible in the opening sentence of Cleanth Brooks' preface to *Modern Poetry and the Tradition* (Chapel Hill, 1939): "Every poet that we read alters to some degree our total conception of poetry."

It must be said that Staiger's dependence upon certain specific phases in literary history for the establishment of general norms narrows the usefulness of his poetics. We must also take issue with general concepts of literary theory which are based largely on a single national literature. Staiger is aware of this difficulty and con-cedes that "In English, in the Romance languages . . . everything looks quite different," [64] and hopefully leaves to the reader the decision whether the principles which he abstracted mainly from examples in German have validity for literature as a whole. But the epilogue to the *Poetik* is less sanguine and seems to indicate a retreat from an early confidence in the universality of the *Grundbegriffe*: "I concede the possibility that everything may be of interest only from a German perspective." [65] Now and then it sounds as though the author were making a kind of last stand from which some day a new offensive could be mounted. "However, the possibility of relevance to world literature seems to remain open." [66]

Staiger's wish would seem to be clear: it is to build a poetics which would embody Heidegger's three existential modes. It would be an "ultimate" poetics concerned not so much with the written or spoken word but rather with ontological analysis. "The concepts lyric, epic, dramatic are designations of literary scholarship con-

---

[63] T. S. Eliot, *Selected Essays*, 3rd ed. (London, 1951), p. 15.
[64] *Poetik*, p. 225.
[65] *Ibid.*, p. 245.
[66] *Ibid.*

cerning fundamental possibilities of human existence; and lyric, epic, and dramatic poetry exist only because the spheres of emotional, figurative, and logical power constitute the essence of man." [67]

The principles dealing with the "essence of man" entail an isolation from the written word which would indeed appear to be a serious shortcoming in any theory that would bring new illumination and order to literature. If the "pure" concept of the "lyrical" is shown to be pre-eminently applicable to some poems by Goethe, Brentano, and Eichendorff, but not to Horace and Petrarch, then —according to Staiger's scheme—Horace and Petrarch must enevitably be "epic" or "dramatic," because that would exhaust all of Staiger's basic modes. We find, however, that Staiger does not account for Petrarch's sonnets nor, for that matter, for Dante's short poems, thus making it impossible for us to know how Staiger's poetics would apply to poetry which, after all, is traditionally classified as lyrical. When confronted by Horace, Staiger reaches an impasse which he cannot overcome by the somewhat curious explanation that Horatian poems are frequently allusive to Greek models and hence do not form a "closed cosmos":

> If we wish to understand Horace, we must take into account that his language does not form the kind of closed cosmos which my *Poetik* attempts to describe, i.e., it vibrates not only within itself but persists in relationship to something different which lies without it. Only in so far as that which lies without —Greek lyric poetry in the case of Horace—constitutes a pure poetic cosmos, is it possible indirectly to engage in an investigation along the lines of my *Poetik*.[68]

Derivative poetry would somehow not be quite representative of the poet's innermost sensibility. Staiger fails to distinguish between the raw material and the structured content of poetry. A poet's style is surely no less individual if he borrows or assimilates lines or elements of plot which occur elsewhere. The impasse resulting from Staiger's reasoning must be considered symptomatic of a flaw in a system depending ultimately on extra-literary absolutes. Staiger wishes to eliminate the confusion inherent in a neo-Aristotelian catalogue of literary kinds and genres, but in fact the confusion arising from the rigorous application of the *Grundbegriffe*

---

[67] *Ibid.*, p. 209.
[68] *Ibid.*, p. 246.

would make the old poetics seem simple by comparison. A work of literature would no longer be discussed and evaluated by referring to its traditional literary genre or kind, but rather it would be viewed as a particular admixture of the three existential modes. Thus it would become very difficult to arrive at a classification of a work, and in such cases where none of the modes appeared to stand out as dominant, no principle of order could be applied; the door to mere impressionistic notions would be left wide open.

Staiger has written highly perceptive and enlightening criticism of individual works of literature, particularly of shorter pieces. His treatments of Mörike's *Auf eine Lampe* and Goethe's *Dauer im Wechsel,* and the masterful stylistic analysis of Kleist's prose piece *Das Bettelweib von Locarno* are models of their kind. The great critical biographies of Goethe[69] and Schiller[70] illuminate the poets' total personalities by drawing light from their works, and not by the reverse process which had hitherto been more common. Only from Staiger's attempts to expand his insights into theoretical principles do certain basic misgivings and objections arise.

In order to judge Staiger's poetics with fairness, it will be necessary to know with some precision just what the characteristics of each of the *Grundbegriffe* are, what specifically is meant by "lyric," "epic," and "dramatic." Staiger states repeatedly that no poem can embody a basic mode in its pure form: language is always at least partially conceptual; its mere presence contradicts the idea of "the lyric," [71] which is the "soul speaking." [72] Moreover, no poem, no matter how "lyrical," can be completely devoid of the epic element, because every meaningful utterance represents or refers to something (*stellt etwas vor*), a characteristic typical of the epic mode. The dramatic element is equally ubiquitous in literature, because it is present in all logical and syntactical relationships. The new classification, according to Staiger, can therefore never be more than an approximation, because to say that a poem is "lyrical" merely refers to the preponderance of one of the three elements over the other.[73]

The "lyric," however, is the ultimate element in any poetic ex-

---

[69] Emil Staiger, *Goethe,* 3 vols. (Zürich, 1952–56).

[70] Emil Staiger, *Friedrich Schiller* (Zürich, 1967).

[71] "[das Gedicht] besteht aus Wörtern, die immer zugleich Begriffe sind. . . aus Sätzen, die immer zugleich einen objectiven Zusammenhand bedeuten. . . ." (*Poetik,* p. 77).

[72] ". . . jenes an sich unmögliche Sprechen der Seele. . . ." (*Ibid.,* p. 78.)

[73] *Ibid.,* p. 10.

pression. Every true poem contains it and no analysis can penetrate beyond it.[74] It is even possible to conceive of a rising curve of poetic modes without thereby insisting on a chronological sequence. Staiger does, however, conceive of the possibility of an historical progression from the lyrical to the dramatic mode, at least of an upward surge and eventual realization of the highest human capacities. Such a development, however, differs from Hegel's dialectic progression in that it is openly hypothetical and antedates any of the literary documents known to us.[75]

The lyrical as the most fundamental mode properly undergoes the most detailed examination by Staiger; attention is given to the author's as well as to the reader's mood, and also to the work itself. Staiger does not explain how he arrives at an analysis of extra-literary factors, but it must be assumed that it is accomplished by extending the mood (*Stimmung*) of the poem in both directions: toward the author on one side and the reader on the other.

Goethe's poem "Wanderers Nachtlied" provides Staiger with a lyric poem par excellence, which allows him to demonstrate and develop some aspects of his own concept of the lyrical mode.

> Über allen Gipfeln
> Ist Ruh,
> In Allen Wipfeln
> Spürest du
> Kaum einen Hauch;
> Die Vögelein schweigen im Walde.
> Warte nur, balde
> Ruhest du auch.

Staiger finds that here—and therefore in all predominantly lyrical poems—there is no imitation of sound, but that the poem has *become* what it represents. Subject and object have become one.[76]

The ideal lyric poem, furthermore, abides by no conventions of meter and rhyme. Each poem is a law unto itself. The orientation is not toward prose but toward a rhythm which is organic to the

---

[74] *Ibid.*, p. 207.

[75] See *ibid.*, p. 211.

[76] "Im lyrischen Stil dagegen wird nicht ein Vorgang sprachlich 'wieder'—gegeben. Es ist nicht so, dass im 'Wanderers Nachtlied' hier die Abendstimmung wäre, und dort die Sprache mit ihren Worten zur Verfügung stünde und auf den Gegenstand angewandt würde. Sondern der Abend erklingt als Sprache von selber. . . ." (*Ibid.*, p. 15.)

poem, and an expression of a feeling-tone.[77] This should not lead
us to believe, however, that a poem written in a conventional meter
would by necessity be unlyrical. Enough variations are possible
within a metric scheme to allow for the minutest changes in *Stimmung*.

The nature of the lyrical poem demands that it be short, for it
represents a single passing moment which is quickly dissipated by
the sobering influence of the matter-of-fact world. The consonance
of the poet with pure lyrical existence is of short duration.[78] For
this view Staiger registers his indebtedness to Hegel's disciple Fr.
Th. Vischer, who in his aesthetics speaks of the world's coming to
a "point of ignition" in the lyrical subject.[79] Thus the advocacy of
shortness for lyrical poetry, which has been of major concern to
modern poetics since Edgar Allan Poe's insistence on it in his
Philosophy of Composition (1846), is reiterated by Staiger in terms
of the poet's inability to sustain the lyrical mode of existence
for any protracted period. It may be that several "points of ignition"
occur in sequence, which results in a longer poem. In such a case
the existential unity of the poem would be broken and it would
consist of a chain of lyrical moments held together by connecting
verses. The latter would serve to indicate the passing of one moment
and set the mood for the succeeding one. Accordingly Staiger
equates the longer lyrical poem with song, and in fact considers
the folk song an almost pure exemplification of the lyric mode in
which the lyrical moments are held together by the refrain. Thus
a primarily lyrical talent like Brentano liked to imitate songs from
Des Knaben Wunderhorn (1806–1808). In Brentano's ballad-like
songs the musical quality of the refrains far outweighs denotative
or even connotative meaning. Repetition, which, according to Staiger
is essential to longer lyrical poems, need not consist of the traditional refrain. Very often it is simply a unique mood which is
sounded again and again by the use of similar words. One of
Staiger's favorite images for the latter type of lyrical repetition is
that of a harp on which the same chord is plucked at regular intervals.[80] Musical impressions supersede a preoccupation with the

---

[77] *Ibid.*, p. 28.

[78] "Jedes Lied ist kurz, weil es nur so lange dauert, als das Seiende mit
dem Dichter übereinstimmt." (*Ibid.*, p. 81.)

[79] "[die lyrische Poesie] ist ein punktuelles Zünden der Welt im Subjekte."
(Fr. Th. Visher, *Werke*, ed. Robert Vischer, 2nd ed. [München, 1923], VI,
208.)

[80] Cf. *Poetik*, pp. 30, 35; also *Zeit*, p. 56.

poetic fact as such. To show the kind of poem which Staiger would call pre-eminently lyrical and to which the specific comments on lyrical repetition apply, we reproduce Brentano's "Spinnerin" from the fragmentary novel *Aus der Chronika eines fahrenden Schülers* (1818):

> Es sang vor langen Jahren
> Wohl auch die Nachtigall,
> Das war wohl süsser Schall,
> Da wir zusammen waren.
>
> Ich sing' und kann nicht weinen
> Und spinne so allein
> Den Faden klar und rein,
> Solang der Mond wird scheinen.
>
> Da wir zusammen waren,
> Da sang die Nachtigall;
> Nun mahnet mich ihr Schall,
> Dass du von mir gefahren.
>
> So oft der Mond mag scheinen,
> Gedenk' ich dein allein;
> Mein Herz ist klar und rein,
> Gott wolle uns vereinen!
>
> Seit du von mir gefahren,
> Singt stets die Nachtigall,
> Ich denk' bei ihrem Schall,
> Wie wir zusammen waren.
>
> Gott wolle uns vereinen,
> Hier spinn' ich so allein
> Der Mond scheint klar und rein,
> Ich sing' und möchte weinen!

Staiger finds that poetic language itself may contain certain important elements characteristic of the lyric mode, despite the fact that its conceptual character and its necessary minimum of syntactical coherence stand in direct opposition to this mode. In a "lyrical" poem, such as the "Spinnerin," syntax will be neglected to a point where sequences of words stand on the borderline between music and language. As a result, language as communication plays a minor role. The mood (*Stimmung*) of a lyric line is so expressive, according to Staiger, that the essence of it may be perceived even by those who are ignorant of the language in which the poem was written.

The allusion to analogy between music and lyrical poetry recalls a romantic conception which M.H. Abrams appropriately labels *Ut Musica Poesis*.[81] John C. Ransom and René Wellek have conclusively shown that sound patterns in poetic language are not to be equated with the patterns of musical sound, and that their meaning cannot be properly interpreted in the absence of denotative or connotative meanings of words, phrases, and contexts.[82] Staiger shows how in certain romantic poems (for example, in Brentano's *Frühe Liedchen* and in *Wie sich auch die Zeit will wenden*) the conceptual meaning is extremely vague and almost non-existent, and that in some cases which perhaps "go a bit too far," musical patterns have replaced such meaning.[83]

In further characterizing lyrical language, Staiger finds that it is essentially paratactic. Certain conjunctions, especially *weil, dass,* and *wenn*, are indicators of a relatively complicated hypotactic sentence structure which in turn suggests a certain complexity of thought. Such complexity is unsuitable for a lyrical feeling-tone, for "singing and thinking are incompatible." [84] Dependent clauses are distinctly "unlyrical." For the sake of demonstration Staiger quotes a poem of Hebbel entitled *Lied* and then alters it to show how it might be more lyrical:

> Komm, wir wollen Erdbeeren pflücken,
> Ist es doch nicht weit Zum Wald,
> Wollen junge Rosen brechen,
> Sie verwelken ja so bald!
>
> Droben jene Wetterwolke,
> Die dich ängstigt, fürcht ich nicht;

---

[81] M. H. Abrams, *The Mirror and the Lamp* (New York, 1953), p. 88.
[82] See Wellek and Warren, *op. cit.*, pp. 146–50; also John Crowe Ransom, *The World's Body* (New York, 1938), pp. 95–97.
[83] "Freilich geht Brentano zu weit. Er hat einige Lieder gedichtet, . . . worin sich der Sinn so bescheiden hinter dem Lautlichen bergen muss, dass sie fast nur noch Solfeggien sind und man statt ihrer wohl ebenso do, re, mi, fa, sol, la, si, do anstimmen könnte." (*Zeit*, p. 41.)
[84] *Poetik*, p. 37.

Nein, sie ist mir sehr willkommen,
Denn die Mittagssonne sticht.

By removing the offending words *doch, ja, nein, denn,* he arrives
at a single stanza which is more song-like and hence more lyrical:

Wir wollen Erdbeeren pflücken,
Es ist nicht weit zum Wald,
Und junge Rosen brechen,
Rosen verwelken so bald. . . .

It is fairly easy to agree with Staiger when he says that paratactic
sentence structure occurs very frequently in German romantic
poetry. We cannot go along with him, however, when he holds
that such a syntactical feature is typical of *all* lyrical poetry. Here
Staiger merely substitutes the adjective "lyric" for "romantic." Such
objections are not effectively met by asserting that the high point
of lyrical style was achieved precisely with German romanticism:
"The objection that such parataxis is characteristic of the romantic
style, is justified only inasmuch as German romanticism reaches
the pinnacle of the song in world literature and hence of the purest
lyric poetry." [85] The changes which Staiger suggests for Hebbel's
poem involve an assumption that the author *intended* to write a
"lyrical" poem, and therefore ought to have adhered to certain
principles. Although Staiger repeatedly emphasizes that his basic
principles as such do not imply, or even permit, value judgments,
we nevertheless see in examples of this type that "lyrical" as well as
the other *Grundbegriffe* almost unnoticeably become aesthetic im-
peratives; for in an ontological system such as Staiger's, the distinction between the author's intention and the completed work of
art is far less clear-cut than in a poetics which limits itself to the
written word. Indeed Staiger's basic concepts need not involve
imaginative writing at all and may be entirely based on the human
experience of nature: "The . . . 'ideal meaning' of 'the lyrical'
may come to me from the experience of a landscape; the 'epic'
perhaps from a stream of refugees; a quarrel may have impressed
on me the idea of the 'dramatic.' " [86] Only we should ask ourselves
whether Staiger may not be reversing cause and effect, because it
must be doubted that such categorized feeling-tones are indeed
inherent in the experience of nature, unless the mind be precon-

---

[85] *Ibid.,* p. 39.
[86] *Ibid.,* p. 9.

ditioned by literature. One is reminded of Oscar Wilde's "Nature imitates art," and Jacques Maritain's acceptance of this principle: ". . . we also see that Oscar Wilde's saying, Nature imitates Art, is but an obvious truism. . . . For man's art and vision too are one of the ways through which mankind invades Nature, so as to be reflected and meant by her." [87]

We tend to resist the notion that the experience of nature be regarded as a poetic principle, and we hold that the "frosty impression" created by Hebbel's poem—one need not quarrel with this observation—does not constitute a failure to adhere to a romantically colored idea of "the lyric." We find instead that such an impression is caused by a superfluity of words and a style inappropriate for a simple, rustic scene and childlike mood. The "unlyrical" conjunctions and the resulting hypotactic sentence structure show a sophistication which is not in keeping with the ingenuousness and simplicity of the situation.

As has been pointed out, Staiger considers the author's state of mind, as well as the effect that a literary work may have on the reader, an integral part of his poetics. Thus he holds that the lyrical utterance requires no effort. It is inspired and not made. The lyrical poet is not a maker but a passive instrument, a harp whose strings vibrate with the breath of inspiration. He is the very image of Plato's ignorant rhapsode Ion, though the latter was interpreting Homeric epic poetry rather then lyrical poetry. All a lyrical poet can do toward achieving his goal is to wait for inspiration. He is "phlegmatic like Mörike" or "will-less like Brentano" while the epic poet is diligent, and the dramatist doggedly determined.[88] The lyric poet is true to his character even if he re-writes and "files" his lines, because he does it only by attuning his ear to the mood once produced.[89] Occasionally, however, Staiger does concede that lyrical poetry may be produced by artifice rather than by inspiration; but this observation in no way induces him to alter his basic assumption with respect to the poet's place within the scheme of lyrical poetry.[90]

Staiger is not only concerned with the mode of existence of the writer, but as well with the effect that a poetic work may have on

---

[87] Jacques Maritain, *Creative Intuition in Art and Poetry* (New York, 1955), p. 8.

[88] *Poetik*, p. 78.

[89] *Ibid.*, p. 24.

[90] *Ibid.*, pp. 78–79.

the reader or listener. Because a lyrical poem cannot be rationally understood, Staiger holds that the public for such poems must necessarily be very small. It occurs relatively rarely that a reader "vibrates" along with the poem and feels a sense of affinity with the poet. Such moments take place only at special hours and during a particular state of mind. Hence a public reading of a lyrical poem is almost always embarrassing; the lyrical moment is the most intimate of all experiences. Lyrical lines "flow" into one's soul, whereas an epic "seizes" the reader or listener, and the drama stirs up and creates suspense.[91]

Staiger feels that many lyrical poems do not achieve their fullest expression until set to music. Music, Staiger asserts, helps to prepare the *Stimmung* and enhances perceptiveness to the vibrations set off by the poem. He shows no concern with the problematical nature of the marriage between music and poetic language. The mutual illumination of the two arts is accepted uncritically.[92] Hugo Wolf, always "bent on the most faithful interpretation" in his music, is therefore considered a superb interpreter of lyrical poetry. Staiger is apparently untroubled by the fact that the transfer of artistic effects from one art to another does not constitute critical interpretation. It would seem to me that by neglecting the need for verbal conceptualization, the literary interpreter can do no more than engage in vague, rhapsodic hints. It is true that in the case of Becking's fanciful representations of rhythm and musical style as configurations of a conductor's beat,[93] Staiger acknowledges that without the reduction of such *Schlagfiguren* into conceptual language the latter remain "undecipherable hieroglyphs," no matter how incisive their suggestiveness.[94] He fails to note, however, that by depending on a musical interpretation of "the lyric" he would

---

[91] "Das ist die Wirkung einer Kunst, die weder, wie die epische, fesselt, noch, wie die dramatische, aufregt und spannt. Das Lyrische wird eingeflösst." (*Ibid.*, p. 48.)

[92] [Schubert, Schumann, Brahms, Hugo Wolf, Schoeck] haben mit ihrer Musik den Menschen deutscher Zunge unermessliche Schätze der lyrischen Dichtung erschlossen, Hugo Wolf zumal, der immer auf treueste Auslegung bedacht ist und kaum je über das Wort des Dichters hinausmusiziert." (*Ibid.*, p. 48.)

[93] See Gustav Becking, *Der Musikalische Rhythmus als Erkenntnisquelle* (Augsburg, 1928), appendix, *et passim*.

[94] "Schlagfiguren sind aber unentzifferte Hieroglyphen ohne den Text, auf den sie sich beziehen. Sie sagen nur dem etwas, der das Gedicht bereits verstanden hat." (*Interpretation*, p. 19.)

be, like Becking, dealing with "hieroglyphs," which cannot yield their conceptual meaning except to those who have previously comprehended it.

Because Staiger's view of the lyric mode has been discussed in some detail, we may now present the other two modes in a more schematic manner.

In analogy to the lyric, each of the other two modes is viewed in its total anthropological and existential context: there is an epic and dramatic state of mind in the reader (*gefesselt* and *gespannt* respectively) as well as in the poet. Both "exist" epically or dramatically. The most epic of poets, Homer, is not involved in the events he describes. The unremitting use of a single meter, in this case the hexameter, points to the author's equanimity and lack of involvement. The distance between the author and the event recounted is always discernible.[95]

The tragic poet, on the other hand, is one whose path leads toward self-destruction. Staiger sees Kleist's life as the model of such a "tragic" existence. The "Nordic harshness of the hypochondriac" is a necessary feature of such a life, as well as unwavering determination to follow through: "Only the inexorably consistent spirit suffers tragedy. But tragedy must necessarily destroy the inexorably consistent spirit, unless weariness spreads a protective twilight over his soul." [96] Analogous to the lyric and epic modes, Staiger sees the dramatic mode as encompassing the "dramatic" author and his public. An interpretation by Staiger of a little prose narrative by Kleist, *Das Bettelweib von Locarno*, ends with a statement that vividly—and dramatically—demonstrates how the "dramatic" mode, like the other modes, engulfs author and reader alike: "... we are so completely possessed by Kleist that only a jolt may finally free us from the entanglement and release us from a human condition whose deadliness is demonstrated by the poet's own end." [97]

For epic poetry as well, it is not abstraction from a large body of poetry that interests Staiger, but rather the work of a single poet, through which he arrives at his concept. It is therefore proper that Homer's *Iliad* and *Odyssey* should reveal the essence of the

---

[95] "Homer steigt aus dem Strom des Daseins empor und steht befestigt, unbewegt den Dingen gegenüber. Er sieht von einem Standpunkt aus, in einer bestimmten Perspektive." (*Poetik*, p. 84.)

[96] *Poetik*, p. 190.

[97] *Meisterwerke deutscher Sprache, op. cit.*, p. 118. Kleist committed suicide in 1811.

epic mode, and it is on this assumption that Staiger proceeds,[98] though even Homeric hexameters may occasionally contain elements other than epic. The *Odyssey* with its "fragrant landscapes" and its "melting colors" often approaches a lyrical quality. Particularly the Nausicaa scenes contain more than a hint of lyricism because "love is not an epical topic inasmuch as it dissolves and melts the contours of individual existence." [99] On the whole, however, it is in Homer that Staiger discovers the criteria characteristic of truly epic poetry. The detachment of the poet is evident not only in the regularity of the meter but also in the fact that in most cases one hexameter corresponds to the length of an ordinary period. As in lyric poetry the syntax is paratactic, but epic parataxis differs radically from lyric parataxis in that is is self-sufficient. Each line is a comprehensible unit, and the poem would not lose its unity if one or the other line were dropped. In a lyrical poem, on the other hand, the lines are so interwoven and so delicately balanced that the removal of one of them might well destroy the poem's total meaning. The structure of an epic poem may therefore be characterized as one of "addition." [100] Lines as well as elements of plot are simply added to one another as self-sufficient units. Staiger makes the controversial assertion that the *Iliad* could be cut to one half or even one third of its original length, and nobody would miss the excised passages unless, of course, he were familiar with the entire work.[101] Such independence and self-sufficiency of the parts pertain not only to the form of the work but also to the relationship among the characters. For example, the relationship of Agamemnon to his subordinates is one of *primus inter pares*. Each of the Hellenic heroes is a great leader in his own right who performs his deeds not out of obedience to a superior but for reasons of his own. The situation is similar among the gods. The lesser gods often object to Zeus' commands and attempt to circumvent them by various ruses.

The clarity of outlines and the attendant abundance of light are not conducive to a merging of the poet with his environment, nor to the "sympathetic vibrations" between poet and reader, as had been observed in lyrical poetry. The kinship between lyrical poetry and music has its analogue in the relationship between epic poetry

---

[98] ". . . ist Homer . . . der einzige Dichter, in dem das Wesen des Epischen noch einigermassen rein erscheint." (*Ibid.*, p. 132.)

[99] *Ibid.*, p. 100.

[100] *Ibid.*, p. 117.

[101] *Ibid.*, p. 116.

and the plastic arts.[102] In the case of music it was necessary to admit that "a fugue by Bach is not lyrical," [103] but we look in vain for a statement that would remind us that certain styles of sculpture or architecture are not at all "epic," if indeed one wished to persist in applying literary terms to architecture.

Accordingly the words in epic poetry are not "cries of feeling" and never lack denotative meaning. While lyric words tend to *become* what they express, the epic phrase *represents* (*vergegenwär-tigt*) something. Lyrical poetry can be compared to pure musical expression, but onomatopoeia, which is typical of epic verse, is indirect and illustrative. It is somewhat akin to program music. The epic poet is always bent on indicating and representing an object or an action. "Epic onomatopoeia is meant to clarify by means of language. The stress everywhere is on clarification, demonstration, and on making things concrete." [104]

The dramatic mode is the third and highest stage of human and poetic development. Leaning on Cassirer's theory of language,[105] Staiger regards the three modes as analogous to progressive stages in the development of language from emotional to logical expression. The first phase of sensuous expression (*sinnlicher Ausdruck*) corresponds to the lyric, concrete expression (*anschaulicher Ausdruck*) to the epic, and conceptual thought and expression (*begriffliches Denken*) to the dramatic mode. The dramatic poet has emerged from the phase of lyrical union between poet, poem and public; he no longer dwells on descriptions of scenes for their own sake, as does the epic poet, but rushes headlong from a point of departure to a fixed goal. "The concern of the poet is not with all points along the line of a movement, as in epic poetry, nor with the quality of the movement, as in lyric poetry, but rather with its destination. Everything depends—in the real sense of the word— upon the end." [106] The dramatic mode thus transcends both the lyric and the epic and reduces them to its premises.[107] But the "dramatic" pervades all literary genres, and the most dramatic work is not necessarily written for the stage. An epigram, a fable, a novelette

---

[102] "Die schöpferische Kraft von Homers Blick bewährt sich zumal in der bildenden Kunst." (*Ibid.*, p. 97.)

[103] *Ibid.*, pp. 52–53.

[104] *Ibid.*, p. 93.

[105] See *Philosophie der symbolischen Formen*, 1. Teil (Berlin, 1923).

[106] *Poetik*, p. 158.

[107] "Damit setzt er [der dramatische Dichter] das Epische zur blossen Voraussetzung herab." (*Ibid.*, p. 167.)

or novel may come closer to being a pure representative of this basic mode than a piece written for the stage. Staiger will have nothing to do with an historical exegesis which would derive dramatic style from the demands of the stage. Because there is no room in an ontological poetics for historical relativism or even perspectivism, he holds that historical causes are dispensable in the realm of pure aesthetics. In rather startling fashion Staiger reverses the traditional causal sequence, and views the institution of the stage as a development made necessary by the demands of the dramatic spirit. "The stage was created out of the spirit of dramatic poetry; it was the only adequate instrument for the new poetry." [108]

When Staiger speaks of dramatic style he refers not only to peculiarities of rhythm and language but also to a tension arising from a "dramatic" *Weltanschauung*, a word which is to be taken in a philosophic, i.e., Heideggerian, sense. *Welt* designates the peculiar relationship of a human mind to that which is perceived by that mind. For example, a peasant views a landscape with respect to its fruitfulness, a military man with respect to its tactical and strategic aspects; a painter will see its lines and colors.[109] The concept of *Welt* could be applied to all three basic modes, since it may be interchanged with "style," so long as the latter is understood in a broad enough manner. "The differences with respect to different *Welten* are differences in style, so that in aesthetics we may without hesitation interchange the expressions "*Welt*" and "style." [110]

The dramatic poet's special way of looking at the world is characterized by a lack of interest in things as such. He is concerned only with their relationship to one another. Things and events are mere signs pointing toward the clarification of an idea or a problem. The question "to what end" (*worumwillen*) constantly imposes itself. The public exposed to the dramatic mode experiences suspense. The dramatic poet himself is "relentless" (*unerbittlich*) and the dramatic style may be either "pathetic" or "problematical." The prepon-

---

[108] *Ibid.*, p. 144.
[109] This is essentially an interpretation and simplification of Heidegger's thinking on the subject of *Welt*. See Heidegger, *Vom Wesen des Grundes*, 4th ed. (Frankfurt, 1955), p. 36: "Vielmehr liegt das metaphysisch Wesentliche der mehr oder minder klar abgehobenen Bedeutung von kosmos, mundus, Welt darin, dass sie auf die Auslegung des menschlichen Daseins *in seinem Bezug zum Seienden im Ganzen abzielt.*"
[110] *Poetik*, p. 173. See also Staiger, "Versuch über den Begriff des Schönen," *Trivium*, III (1945), 189 ff.

derance of either the dramatic or the lyric states of being are pathological and of limited duration. Brentano—according to Staiger one of the most "lyrical" poets—can maintain neither the wholeness of his life nor the quality of his poetry. Both "fritter away." And Kleist is destroyed by the irreconcilable conflicts inherent in his "dramatic" existence.

Once Staiger has dismissed the relevance of historical development and explained tragedy by resorting to metaphysical, tragic modes of existence, it is only slightly less surprising that he is able to show how basic conventions and norms in tragedy derive their value not from tradition but from the demands of an existential category. In a preponderantly "pathetic" or passionate tragedy everything depends on the force and stature of the protagonist, whose speech must have sufficient impact to overcome the resistance of the public and of his own particular humanity.[111] The importance of pathos is so great that psychological finesse and motivations are out of place. This, rather than an adherence to a convention, is the reason for the traditional demand that the tragic hero be physically elevated, sociologically distinct from the mass and superior to it.

If the drama or tragedy is "problematic," that is if it moves directly toward the solution of an ultimate problem—without distracting epic description or lyrical evocations of mood—then the unremitting concentration demanded of the public is of decisive importance. The attention is exclusively directed toward an ultimate solution to the problem. Any distraction from this goal will relax the tension and make it likely that one or the other incident essential to the forward movement of the plot may be forgotten. It is from such high demands on the public that Staiger derives the justification for the unities of time, place, and action.[112]

There is no doubt that Staiger's scheme of poetic modes is rooted in Hegelian dialectics, although Hegel regards the epic rather than the lyric as the most fundamental mode,[113] and his poetics is far more

---

[111] "Das Pathos wirkt nicht so diskret. Es setzt einen Widerstand voraus, offene Feindschaft oder auch Trägheit, und versucht, ihn mit Nachdruck zu brechen." (*Ibid.*, p. 147.) See also *Poetik*, p. 150: "Wenn das Pathos aber echt ist, erleidet auch der Redner Gewalt."

[112] *Ibid.*, p. 162.

[113] See Friedrich Hegel, *Sämtliche Werke*, ed. Hermann Glockner (Stuttgart, 1928), XIV, 322.

historically oriented than Staiger's.[114] As we have seen (see above, p. 82) Staiger despairs of ever finding historical evidence for his ontological triad, though his thought clearly implies that the sequence lyric-epic-dramatic is historically as well as ideologically sound. Like Hegel, Staiger considers the dramatic the highest possible development in literature, and like Hegel he relates the epic and lyric modes to sculpture and music respectively.[115] In both Hegel and Staiger the lyric and epic are prerequisites to the dramatic mode.[116] For both, drama is the ultimate possibility in the realm of poetry, although Staiger does not envisage (as Hegel does) a human development wherein art in general, and poetry as its highest manifestation, will be transcended and ultimately pass into the realm of pure philosophy.[117]

It is the proper assignment of time dimensions which to Staiger represents the final justification for regarding the three basic kinds of poetry as fundamental and existential. Time forms the center of Heidegger's ontology, and it is from there that Staiger must build the bridge toward a poetics. His first exposition of the role of time for literary modes came in *Die Zeit als Einbildungskraft des Dichters* (1939). In this early work, no attempt is as yet made to press the three traditional kinds of poetry into an analogous existential time scheme. It is an elaborate textual analysis of three German poems (Brentano, "Auf dem Rhein"; Goethe, "Dauer im Wechsel"; Keller, "Die Zeit geht nicht"), which focuses on time as a pure, "concrete" concept (*reine Anschauungsform*). There is a progression from a surging flux of time (*reissende Zeit*) in which the poet is totally involved, to a separation and removal from time, permitting its conscious contemplation (*ruhende Zeit*).

Staiger first points to an overwhelming present time, as in Brentano's image of a dreamy fisherman carried downstream toward the sea and to his death.

He then singles out Goethe's poetic yearning to seize the fleeting moment in "Dauer im Wechsel":

> Hielte diesen frühen Segen
> Ach, nur eine Stunde fest!

---

[114] Hegel's elaborate system in which history and theory imply each other is scrutinized and explained by René Wellek in his *A History of Modern Criticism* (New Haven, 1955), II, 318–34.

[115] Hegel, XIV, 322.

[116] *Ibid.*, XIV, 323–24.

[117] Hegel, XII, 32.

and to gain perspective and freedom by stepping out of the stream of time.

> Lass den Anfang mit dem Ende
> Sich in Eins zusammenziehn!
> Schneller als die Gegenstände
> Selber dich vorüberfliehn!

And last he sees in Keller a crystallization of time into a static eternity:

> Die Ziet geht nicht, sie stehet still,
> Wir ziehen durch sie hin;
> Sie ist ein Karawanserei,
> Wir sind die Pilger drin.

According to Staiger, the triadic obsession of German idealism is rooted in an intuitive perception of time as the ultimate form of existence. The three dimensions of time, or *Ekstasen* in Heidegger's terminology, may be found in a multiplicity of triads, most significantly perhaps in the division of the arts into music, plastic arts, and poetry. It must be understood that for Heidegger's *Ekstasen*, grammatical tense is not of the essence; nor is the objective concept of time, as used in the natural sciences, of particular concern to the Staiger-Heidegger system. What does matter is the *reine Anschauung*, through which the three modes of poetry must reveal themselves as fundamental modes of existence. The poet, while composing poetry, "exists" predominantly in one mode. His existence is "purer" in the act of composition than in his daily, unpoetic life. It therefore becomes incumbent upon Staiger to equate the poetic kinds with the three *Ekstasen* of time. Throughout his *Grundbegriffe der Poetik* he works toward this equation, and in the final chapters it becomes explicit in the form: lyric is past time; epic is present time; drama is future time. It is obvious that the gulf between Heidegger's ontology and Staiger's poetic modes is difficult to bridge, and the impression of arbitrariness is not easily dispelled. Similar temporal schemes had been worked out by others, but there has been no agreement regarding the proper distribution of the triad past-present-future. Probably the earliest scheme of this type was proposed by Jean Paul. (See note 46.) The post-romantic English critic, E. S. Dallas, associates lyric with future, epic with past, and drama with present time.[118] Fr. Th. Vischer suggests the past

---

[118] E. S. Dallas, *Poetics: An Essay on Poetry* (London, 1852), pp. 81, 105.

for epic poetry, the present for the lyric, and the future for drama.[119] John Erskine interpreted the three literary kinds as types of poetic temperament and regards the lyric as present, and curiously, the epic as future and drama as past.[120]

It would seem that if one were asked to render an intuitive judgment, one would naturally assign present time to the kind of romantic poetry which to Staiger is representative of the lyric mode. Indeed Staiger notes that the grammatical present tense is dominant in lyrical poetry. When discussing the thoroughly "lyrical" poem "Auf dem Rhein" by Brentano, he emphasizes the absence of a past or future and the dominating power of the "now" over the fisherman.[121] The lyrical poem—in close analogy to music—evokes and *becomes* the mood or *Stimmung* of one particular moment.[122] The poet is steeped in that mood and can therefore only dwell in immediate experience. Yet Staiger assigns not present but past time to the lyric mode. It must be remembered that, according to Heidegger, only that which *has been* (*die Gewesenheit*, see above, p. 83n) makes this *Stimmung* possible. One has the feeling that, under an inner compulsion to make his poetics conform to Heidegger's ontology, Staiger strains his evidence by an ingenious manipulation of terms. The title of the first chapter of Staiger's *Grundbegriffe der Poetik* is "Lyrischer Stil: Erinnerung." The "carrying inward" implied by the word *Erinnerung* is shown to be the essence of the lyrical mode. Staiger's penchant for making the original meaning of a word's component parts serve the purpose of conceptual elucidation has been pointed out (see above, pp. 85–86). It has also been shown how sometimes the original and the current meanings are used alternately and serve Staiger to demonstrate the correctness of a philosophical insight. In this manner the word *erinnern* is made to serve as a plausible reminder that lyric poetry is "inward" (pointing to the literal and original meaning). Then by implicitly appealing to the current dictionary meaning "to remember," the pastness of the lyric mode is demonstrated. It is therefore possible for Staiger, by using the sense of "to bring inward," to assert that *erinnern* may

---

[119] Fr. Th. Vischer, VI, 123.

[120] John Erskine, *The Kinds of Poetry* (New York, 1920), p. 12.

[121] "Er ist ein Jetzt und nichts als ein Jetzt und fällt so jedem Jetzt anheim." (*Zeit*, p. 67.)

[122] Staiger makes use of an elaboration of the concept of Stimmung by O. F. Bollnow, *Das Wesen der Stimmungen* (Frankfurt, 1941), pp. 17–36.

refer to past, present, and future time,[123] and simultaneously to claim "obvious preterital significance" for the word.[124] It is clear that such "obviousness" must refer to the current meaning of *erinnern*. There are also allusions to a "return to the womb," poetically evoking a primordial condition of lyrical "pastness." [125]

A similar procedure is used by Staiger for the purpose of identifying the epic mode with present time. Tradition as well as a general sensibility would undoubtedly connect the epic with past time, as in fact all of Staiger's predecessors in this field, with the exception of John Erskine, had done. The epic as a distillation of memory would naturally seem to belong to the category of the past. For Staiger, the key word characterizing the epic mode is *vergegenwärtigen*,[126] which means "to represent," "to make real," and when converted into the noun *Gegenwart*, signifies "present time." What the lyric poet "carries inward" the epic poet "represents" or "makes real." [127] Because the German noun *Gegenwart* conveniently may yield one of the important words which Staiger uses to characterize the epic, it becomes linguistically plausible that present time and "the epic" become two aspects of the same mode of existence.

Having determined the time dimensions of two of the basic modes, one can assume the equation dramatic-future to be self-evident. There is no single word which serves Staiger as an indicator of that which is characteristic of the dramatic and at the same time would yield the meaning of futurity. However, the adjectives *spannend* and above all *problematisch*, whose original Greek meaning is "that which is thrown forward," are shown to point to the future, although they do not actually signify futurity.[128]

Such capricious and imaginative manipulation of meanings and connotations is fruitful and suggestive but, as has been indicated, it does not constitute convincing argumentation. If one were to point to the fundamental nature of Staiger's modes of being and to argue that it is not surprising that the three existential modes should be

---

[123] "Gegenwärtiges, Vergangenes, ja sogar Künftiges kann in lyrischer Dichtung erinnert werden." (*Poetik*, p. 62.)

[124] "Dagegen kommt jetzt dem Erinnern offenbar präteritale Bedeutung zu." (*Ibid.*, p. 218.)

[125] "Das lyrische Erinnern jedoch ist Rückkehr in den Mutterschoss in *dem* Sinn, dass ihm alles wieder in jenem Zustand erscheint, aus dem wir aufgestanden sind." (*Ibid.*)

[126] *Ibid.*, pp. 87, 218, 219, *et passim.*

[127] *Ibid.*, p. 218.

[128] *Ibid.*, p. 160.

reflected in language, one would have to point to other words, such as *Vergangenheit* and *Zukunft*, which are not so susceptible to the particular double interpretation which Staiger seeks. By such a method, moreover, Staiger makes himself a prisoner of his own language. Surely a fundamental poetics which derives to any important extent from an interpretation of one's own language—to the exclusion of other important languages—is unlikely to lend itself to universal application.

It will be of interest to examine how Staiger proposes to apply his poetic principles to practical criticism. We must remember that the triad lyric-epic-dramatic does not refer to the traditional categories. Yet Staiger is not quite prepared to say that basic styles, or "rhythms," or *Welten*, have nothing at all to do with the traditional kinds of epic, dramatic, and lyric poetry. On the contrary, he is forced to concede, somewhat reluctantly it appears, that such a connection does indeed exist.[129] This is an important concession in Staiger's poetics, although it appears only in the epilogue written two years after the body of the book. It is here that the possibility of an evaluative criticism appears. Hitherto Staiger had frequently emphasized that the relative purity or impurity of a mode, as it appears in a particular poem, should in no way be indicative of the poem's literary value. But once he concedes that there must be some connection between the *Grundbegriffe* and the traditional kinds of poetry, he is able to make his appeal to a literary institution and to its conventions. It is of no consequence that he refers not to the institutions themselves but to a general area surrounding them. "And thus, working with the concept of spatial latitude, it seems to me to be completely in order to append a long, normative poetics to the *Grundbegriffe* and to throw open the question: What constitutes the space of the ode, the elegy, the novel, comedy?" [130] At this juncture it becomes necessary for Staiger to grant that a narration in verse of considerable length should properly be regarded as something akin to an epic.[131] And indeed the concluding pages of the epilogue contain unequivocal value judgments which cannot readily be reconciled with frequent previous assertions that such evalua-

---

129 Denn wenn man mich nun fragen wollte: Besteht also gar kein Zusammenhang zwischen dem Epos und dem Epischen, der Lyrik und dem Lyrischen mehr, so würde ich mich nicht getrauen, vorbehaltlos zu erwiedern; 'Nein! Es besteht überhaupt kein Zusammenhang.'" (*Ibid.*, p. 248.)

130 *Ibid.*, p. 249.

131 "Kann eine längere Verserzählung auch alles andere sein also episch? Das würde ich schwerlich zugestehen." (*Ibid.*, p. 248.)

tions are not within the scope of his poetics. Thus Klopstock's *Messias* fails to satisfy, because the "epic space has been transgressed" by a mass of lyric and pathetic lines.[132] Gottfried Keller's poems are criticized for opposite reasons. They are too short for the epic imagination properly to unfold itself.[133]

In the end, therefore, Staiger's *Grundbegriffe* are used as instruments of evaluation. "Lyric," "epic," and "dramatic" become attributes of style which may or may not be appropriate to one of the traditional kinds or genres. As an analysis of basic literary styles, Staiger's approach is rich and suggestive. As a basic poetics, however, it moves in a circle and ends with an admission that the traditional poetic kinds and genres have not yet been superseded. The insuperable impasse at which Staiger finds himself becomes evident when he proposes a poetics dealing with the existing possibilities within the general area of traditional genres; he is forced to concede that the task of developing such a prescriptive poetics would be too complex, too difficult, and its validity too ephemeral to make it worthwhile. He prefers to move directly from his *Grundbegriffe* to the interpretation of individual poems,[134] and hereby reinforces the impression that while he has deepened and sharpened our perception of certain important styles of imaginative writing, the foundation for a new poetics has not truly been laid.

In his more recent writings Staiger has shown no interest in reinforcing or extending the system proposed in his poetics. It appears from the essay "Kunst der Interpretation," written in 1951, that he is now moving along different paths. He does not proceed from the *Grundbegriffe* directly to an interpretation, as he had proposed in 1948, but instead allows his analysis to be guided by his talent and musical sensibility, as well as by "historical resonances." [135] There is more than a hint in Staiger's essay that the abandonment of his own theoretical principles is deliberate and that he is not disturbed by the dangers of impressionistic criticism and a resulting relativism. It is significant with respect to Staiger's present position that he now believes the appeal to aesthetic absolutes, whether tra-

---

132 *Ibid.*

133 *Ibid.*, p. 249.

134 "Nur möchte ich mich weigern, dieses Geschäft zu übernehmen. Denn die Verhältnisse scheinen mir hier so kompliziert und schwierig zu sein, so gross ist mein Glaube a neue, ganz unerwartete Möglichkeiten der Dichter, dass ich von den Grundbegriffen lieber gleich zur Interpretation des einzelnen Kunstwerks übergehe." (*Ibid.*, p. 249.)

135 *Interpretation*, p. 16.

ditional or philosophical, to be conducive to unwarranted prejudice. "I am convinced that . . . complete dedication to the objects at hand offers the best possibility of overcoming those schematic classifications which produce so many prejudices and which prevent us from reading . . . what is actually there." [136]

The most valuable judgments appear to arise from a delicate state of suspension and a supreme awareness on the part of the critic, who is then in a position to render full account of all reponses to a literary work without being submerged or governed by them. Such a state in no way obscures a personal perspective but on the contrary is conducive to that reponsiveness and sensitivity for which we look in the best works of criticism.

We noted earlier that merely to identify Scherer with determinism, Walzel with formalism, and Staiger with existentialism would not do justice either to the scope of their theories or to the range of their critical writings. Scherer often rather precariously combined romantic primitivism with scientific determinism. Walzel tried, not very successfully, to unite his formalism with sociological and psychological systems of norms. Staiger makes a fascinating attempt to conceptualize and structure a modern literary sensibility rooted in Heideggerian existentialism and German romanticism. Yet even when given ample play, the three theories emerge as distinctly different approaches to literature, each seeking values which the other two are not equipped to find.

Scientific determinism—as a literary theory—has lost its attractiveness for modern critics, although as a common-sense methodology of practical criticism it still shows surprising strength. In its most fruitful form, extraliterary data are adduced in order to place literary works into proper perspective. At its worst, the examination of a text degenerates into irrelevant discussions of biographical facts and anecdotes.

While morphological criteria derived from the visual arts may not be altogether convincing in literature, Walzel's strenuous efforts toward making a vocabulary of formal terms available to literary criticism were a harbinger of later, more influential endeavors in that direction among groups like the Prague linguistic circle in Europe and the New Critics in the United States. Walzel's formal

---

[136] *Ibid.*, p. 30.

analysis of period-styles and of Shakespearean tragedies provided an important methodological stimulus at a time when the dominant tendency in Germany was to view literature primarily as a vehicle for the expression of the spiritual content of an historical period.

By proposing to merge existential philosophy with literary theory, Staiger has expressed a growing demand in our own day for an ontology of literature. To see the basic literary forms as "modes of being" carries much conviction and is more suggestive than are theories that see only the accidents of tradition and conventions at work in the development of literary genres.

BIBLIOGRAPHY

I. Works by Emil Staiger

"Ein Briefwechsel mit Martin Heidegger," *Trivium*, IX (1951), 1–16; reprinted in *Die Kunst der Interpretation*, pp. 34–49.

"Dialektik der Grundbegriffe Originalität und Nachahmung," in *Tradition und Ursprünglichkeit*, ed. W. Kohlschmidt and H. Meyer (Bern, 1966).

Goethe, 3 vols. (Zürich, 1959).

Grundbegriffe der Poetik, 3rd ed. (Zürich, 1956).

"Hölderlin-Forschung während des Krieges," *Trivium*, IV (1946), 202–19.

Die Kunst der Interpretation, (Zürich, 1955).

"Literatur und Öffentlichkeit," speech delivered in Zürich on Dec. 17, 1966. In *Neue Zürcher Zeitung*, Dec. 18, 1966.

Meisterwerke deutscher Sprache, 2nd ed. (Zürich, 1948).

Musik und Dichtung (Zürich, 1947).

Friedrich Schiller (Zürich, 1967).

Stilwandel, *Studien zur Vorgeschichte der Goethezeit* (Zürich, 1963).

"Versuch über den Begriff des Schönen," *Trivium*, III (1945), 185–97.

Die Zeit als Einbildungskraft des Dichters (Zürich, 1939).

II. Sources and Secondary Readings

Abrams, M.H., *The Mirror and the Lamp* (New York, 1953).

Becking, Gustav, *Der musikalische Rhythmus als Erkenntnisquelle* (Augsburg, 1928).

Behrens, Irene, "Die Lehre von der Einteilung der Dichtkunst," *Beihefte zur Zeitschrift für romanische Philologie*, XCII (1940), 1–252.

Binswanger, Ludwig, *Grundformen und Erkenntnis menschlichen Daseins* (Zürich, 1942).

Bollnow, O.F., *Das Wesen der Stimmungen* (Frankfurt, 1941).

Brentano, Clemens, *Sämtliche Werke*, ed. C. Schüddekopt (München, 1909).

Brooks, Cleanth, *Modern Poetry and the Tradition* (Chapel Hill, 1939).

Cassirer, Ernst, *Die Philosophie der symbolischen Formen* (Berlin, 1923).

Croce, Benedetto, *Aesthetic*, tr. Douglas Ainslee (New York, 1955).

Dallas, E.S., *Poetics: An Essay on Poetry* (London, 1852).

Dilthey, Wilhelm, *Gesammelte Schriften* (Berlin, 1922–36).

Donohue, James J., *The Theory of Literary Kinds* (Dubuque, Iowa, 1943).

Duroche, Leonard L., *Aspects of Literary Criticism in Present-Day Germany* (The Hague, 1967).

Eliot, T.S., *Selected Essays*, 3rd ed. (London, 1951).

Ermatinger, Emil, "Das Gesetz in der Literaturwissenschaft," *Philosophie der Literaturwissenschaft*, ed. Emil Ermatinger (Berlin, 1930), pp. 331–75.

Erskine, John, *The Kinds of Poetry* (New York, 1930).

Gelley, A., "Staiger, Heidegger and the Task of Criticism," *Modern Language Quarterly*, XXIII (1962), 195–216.

Goethe, Johann Wolfgang von, *Sämtliche Werke, Jubiläumsausgabe in 40 Bänden* (Stuttgart, 1902–7).

Hartl, Robert, *Versuch einer psychologischen Grundlegung der Dichtungsgattungen* (Wien, 1924).

Hegel, Georg Wilhelm Friedrich, *Sämtliche Werke*, ed. Hermann Glockner (Stuttgart, 1928).

Heidegger, Martin, *Erläuterungen zu Hölderlins Dichtung* (Frankfurt, 1951).

———, *Sein und Zeit* (Halle a.d.S., 1929).

———, *Vom Wesen des Grundes*, 4th ed. (Frankfurt, 1955).

Hobbes, Thomas, *Critical Essays of the Seventeenth Century*, ed. J. E. Spingarn (Oxford, 1908).

Joyce, James, *A Portrait of the Artist as a Young Man* (New York, 1958).

Kelletat, Alfred, rev. of Emil Staiger, *Grundbegriffe der Poetik*, *Euphorion*, XLVII (1953), 220–24.

Levin, Harry, "Literature as an Institution," *Accent*, VI (1946), 159–69.

Maritain, Jacques, *Creative Intuition in Art and Poetry* (New York, 1955).

Minkowski, E., *Le temps vécu* (Paris, 1936).

Müller, Günther, "Bemerkungen zur Gattungspoetik," *Philosophischer Anzeiger*, III (1929), 129–47.

Novalis (Friedrich von Hardenberg), *Schriften*, ed. Kluckhohn (Leipzig, 1929).

Paul, Jean (Johann Paul Richter), *Sämtliche Werke,* ed. Eduard Berend (Berlin, 1909).

Petersen, Julius, *Die Wissenschaft von der Dichtung* (Berlin, 1939).

Petsch, Robert, "Goethe und die Naturformen der Dichtung," *Dichtung und Forschung, Festschrift für Emil Ermatinger,* (Frauenfeld, 1933).

Poe's Critical Essays, F.C. Prescott ed. (Ithaca, 1909).

Ransom, John Crowe, *The World's Body* (New York, 1938).

Schelling, F.W.J., *Sämtliche Werke,* 14 vols. (Berlin, 1856–61).

Friedrich Schlegel: seine Prosaischen Jugendschriften, ed. J. Minor, 2 vols. (Wien, 1882).

Spitzer, Leo, "Wiederum Mörickes Gedicht 'Auf eine Lampe,'" *Trivium,* IX (1951), 133–47.

Vico, Giambattista, *The New Science,* tr. T.G. Bergin and M.H. Fisch (Ithaca, 1948).

Viëtor, Karl, "Die Geschichte der literarischen Gattungen," *Geist und Form* (Bern, 1952).

Vischer, Friedrich Th., *Werke,* ed. Robert Vischer (München, 1923).

Wellek, René, *A History of Modern Criticism,* 2 vols. (New Haven, 1955).

——, "Concepts and Structure in Twentieth Century Criticism," *Neophilologus,* XXXXII, 1 (1958), 2–11.

Wellek, René and Austin Warren, *Theory of Literature,* 2nd rev. ed. (New York, 1955).

Wilkinson, Elizabeth M., rev. of Emil Staiger, *Grundbegriffe der Poetik, Modern Language Review,* XLIV (1949), 433–37.

INDEX

Abrams, M. H., 3, 101
Andrian-Werburg, Leopold (Walzel's student), 40, 56
Anschauungsformen (Wölfflin's "modes of seeing"), 60–62
Aristotle, 23, 26, 27, 49, 51, 90
Auerbach, Berthold (novelist), 32

Batteux, Charles, 51
Becking, Gustav, 81, 104–5
Behrens, Irene, 90
Benda, Oskar, 44n, 45
Berlin, Academy of, 6, 32
Berlin, University of, 9, 40
Bern, University of, 41
Bismarck, Prince Otto von, 2, 41
Boas, George, 15n, 72
Boeckh, Philip August, 12–13
Bollnow, O. F.: on *Stimmung*, 112n
Bonn, Friedrich: on Scherer-school, 34n
Bonn, University of, 41–42
Boretius, Alfred (jurist), 6
Brentano, Clemens, 88, 96; *Des Knaben Wunderhorn*, 99; "Spinnerin," 100
Brooks, Cleanth: on literary tradition, 95
Bruno, Giordano, 49
Buckle, Henry Thomas, 18–19, 20, 29

Cassirer, Ernst, 107
Categories, literary: as modes of being, 90; as anthropological absolutes, 93; as institutions, 94
Catholicism: church, 10; Walzel's commitment to, 39, 70
Causality, 18, 21–22
Causation, mechanistic or scientific, 3, 46
Church: opposition to the, 12; spirit of the, 12
Cicero, 51–52
Circle, logical (hermeneutic), 92–93
Classicism, German, 49
Compounds, Staiger's separation of, 85–86
Comte, Auguste, 15, 29
Content. See *Gehalt*
Corneille, Pierre, 67
Criticism: American, 4; practical, in Staiger, 114–16
Croce, Benedetto, 89
Cyclic movements, in literature, 15

Dallas, Eneas Sweetland, 111
Dante: terzinas, 50; *Divine Comedy*, 89; short poems, 96
Darwin, Charles, 20, 29
Decorative principle, in Wölfflin, 62
Definitions, Scherer's avoidance of, 27
Dehmel, Richard, 44
Determinism, scientific, 2, 14, 46
Dilthey, Wilhelm, 3, 6, 9, 24, 26, 29–30, 31, 34, 40, 45, 46–48, 92; his "three types," see *Weltanschauung*